Defending the Innocent against Child Protective Services

By

Derek William Bootle MS, MBA

Acknowledgements

The acknowledgements in this book are more difficult than usual due to the topic of the book, and the fear CPS produces in people. After discussing with everybody who helped me, most didn't want their name on or associated with this book, even if only for helping me edit. All people who assisted me are afraid of reprisal from Child Protective Services. None of the people helping with this book have any history of CPS involvement but feel that speaking out against such a nefarious government entity could bring hostility and retribution from an organization designed to destroy families or at the very least contact the IRS and receive a punishment audit.

To the people listed in the book, I am grateful you have allowed me to publish your stories even if the outcomes were not always positive. I am sorry CPS decided to interfere with your lives and made such terrible decisions and actions. I am dedicating this book to every innocent person who has been wrongfully accused and prosecuted by Child Protective Services in your honor.

A big thank you to my wife and kids who put up with me while writing this book. When writing a book, nothing is an individual endeavor, and your love carried me through. Thank you to all my friends who read, proofread, re-proof read, and an especially heartfelt thank you to those who read it and gave excellent feedback. I'm a terrible writer, and I only was able to write this with your help. Thank you to my publisher who allowed my message to be heard.

Derek Bootle MS, MBA

1. Introduction.

There is a government agency (in America) with the power to take your children. Its agents can enter your home and forcefully remove your children without giving cause or reason. When you report this agency to the police, the police support them, not you, not your kids. This agency is under the assumption that it is doing the "public good" protecting children and assisting families. However, they act without thinking, use strong-arm tactics to get information, lie to family court judges and manipulate people to obtain the outcome they desire. The removed children are sold to foster families for between $4000 and $6000 each, depending on whether the child has special needs or disabilities. When they come for your child, there is little recourse for you, and every legal process is against you. This agency will use force and threat of arrest, jail, and violence to obtain the outcome they desire. They will use your financial situation, education, race, religion and legal history against you.

This book will discuss evidence derived from personal accounts, video account, and in-depth personal interviews. This agency, which receives funding from the federal government to identify children to be adopted out and force families to break up, in order to obtain money. This agency is CPS (Child Protective Services). They may have a different acronym in your state, (DCYF), (DYFS), but they are the same agency. For the sake of clarity, I will refer to all state child "protection" agencies as CPS.

Do not hold my opinion as legal or psychological advice. What I am explaining in this book are situations concerning CPS, and the aggressive prosecution made when opening a case with a family, how those situations were managed, the mistakes made in defending those cases and what should be done for a better outcome and maintaining family cohesion. I am presenting them as individual cases which should not be considered in connection with any situation you or someone else may be involved. Every name has been changed for confidentiality. Even if you find the cases helpful, always listen to legal counsel regarding your situation before choosing what to do next, don't rely solely on a book for your defense.

Much of what CPS does is illegal, unconstitutional, unethical and blatantly criminal. Child Protective Services is a state government agency with quasi-police powers, access to sympathetic judges, no accountability for error, fraud, or malfeasance. There is no appeal process, and CPS opinion carries equal weight in court as physical evidence. Child Protective Services have complete power over their choices and fear no one. Child Protective Services hide behind the confidentiality of the child to mask their illegal actions and disapprove of being questioned about their decisions. CPS is so powerful that even the highest politicians will not cross them, as a report "leaked" from CPS can destroy a person's credibility, career, and livelihood.

Child Protective Service agents may come to your door or your child's school after someone places an anonymous call regarding the health and safety of your child. Many people are mandated reporters. People who are obligated by law to report any suspicious behavior, regardless whether they believe they are doing the right thing; and will receive severe punishments including license revocation, jail, and fines if they do not contact CPS to protect themselves from liability.

When hearing of stories regarding CPS intervention the populace usually take the position, "well, they probably did something to the child.", or "they must have had good reason to investigate." This is not always the case. Often the actions of CPS is about money, but sometimes it is personal. Two instances I present in this book will document how CPS not only took it personally but aggressively attacked the families.

Over the past 20 years or so, I've worked in various community mental health centers and hospitals all over the country. As a psychiatric clinician and therapist, I've worked with hundreds of families in several states. One of my duties was working with families with Child Protective Services involvement who also had mental illnesses and various other social problems, which cause the state agency to become involved in their care. Over time I've learned many different things regarding CPS, including that the agents do not always get the case right, as errors often occur in the system. When this happens, a great injustice occurs, ultimately to the destruction of families
and the detriment of the psychological health of children.

Child Protective Services is a vital part of today's society and the children who need protection from abuse. Abuse is a grave matter and warrants serious consequences. However mistakes can be made, money is an incentive to dissolve parental rights, or if the overzealous nature of the CPS agent comes into play, it can be more traumatizing to the child for CPS to become involved, than the actual abuse.

The information I have learned over the years through my dealings with Child Protective Services as a counselor is vital to develop a defense from false prosecutions. Many attorneys are not aware of this information developed from my different role as an outsider's view of the parent, child, and CPS. We need to open a dialogue regarding false positives in the Child Protective Services system and discuss ideas into how to change CPS' focus, techniques, and culture.

Lastly, I've had numerous people outside of the mental health arena, ask for help regarding issues with CPS. These people include single moms, single dads, and friends of the family. This contact has proven an immense need for this information to become public.

Working for Child Protective Services is a challenging job. Child Protective Services has a limited state-funded budget, overloaded caseloads, and dealing with the public under some disgusting situations. A significant part of the problem with Child Protective Services is that having a such a limited state-budget, this requires it to use other methods to gain funding. The Adoption and Child Safety Act provide a revenue stream to be exploited to maintain and grow CPS' budgets. This funding is sourced by on taking children from their homes, placing them with foster families, and then adopting them out. It sounds unbelievable that something like this could happen in modern day America, but it happens on a daily basis to people who have done nothing more than given the wrong information to the CPS agent.

The Adoption and Child Safety Act signed by President Bill Clinton in 1997 was meant to expedite the adoption of children living from foster care into stable families. As you look at the legal title of this law, it appears benign, but it is sinister in its focus. The law decreases the time between when the investigation and child removal from 18 months to 12 months, and develop subsidies from Title IV-B and Title IV-E to Child Protective Services as motivation to speed up the process. These subsidies provide $4000-$6000 stipends to Child Protective Services from the United States Federal Budget for every child removed from one family's care into a foster or adoptive home.

On its face, the subsidy appears to be a small amount provided to the state, but when multiplied by a relatively small number like 20, you can see how a $4000 stipend turns into $80,000 fairly quickly. If you consider the numbers as one year, 200 children removed equals nearly $1,000,000 of extra funding. According to (Children's rights.org), "On any given day, there are nearly 428,000 children in foster care in the United States. In 2015, more than 62,000 children- whose mothers' and fathers' parental rights had been legally terminated- were waiting to be adopted." When you provide a monetary benefit to any action, you are going to see an increase of that action. We have seen it over the past 20 years, a dramatic rise in child removal and adoption, strong-arm tactics, and forced removal for the slightest of "offenses" as getting a second opinion on a medical issue, dirty dishes in the sink, not seeking medical care for a cold, etc.

2. Dave and Sonya.

Dave and Sonya were an unmarried couple (common law marriage) in their early 20's. Sonya was the mother of a baby girl (Jill) with Dave. They lived in a multiple family house outside of Providence Rhode Island. Both were on social security disability. Sonya had mild to moderate mental delays, and Dave had bipolar disorder with psychotic features. Both were on medications and seeing mental health professionals for their issues. Both parents were good people who were warm and loving to their daughter. Their income was barely enough to cover the necessities such as food, rent, and clothes. They were receiving assistance from Women, Infant, and Children otherwise known as (WIC) food support program for Jill. The house was cluttered and old, with age and poor upkeep showing in the walls and ceiling. It was not ideal, but it was warm, they liked it, and they loved each other.

Dave was referred to our team at the mental health agency after a manic episode, where Emergency Medical Services (EMS) was contacted by his neighbors due to his frequent outbursts, staying up all night, delusions, and paranoia. He had suffered from this illness for a few years, but it had never manifested itself in such a severe way before. He was not on any medications and was very sick. After being assessed by EMS, Child Protective Services was contacted to determine whether the mother could manage the baby on her own. CPS considered removed the baby from Sonya's care based on Dave's actions and Sonya's disability. Sonya was utterly overwhelmed by the commotion from Dave, CPS, and EMS.

During that time, Dave in his paranoid and delusional state made several claims about running away, taking the baby, doing harm to himself, and had also threatened the social worker. Emergency removal of the child was made for the child's safety. Dave was placed in a psychiatric hospital to stabilize his symptoms and to administer medications. Dave was released after spending two weeks in the hospital with no notable manic or psychotic features. Depakote and Haldol (medications) worked well to manage his symptoms. He applied to our community mental health clinic for continuing care. Care included: medication management, psychiatrist visits, daily symptom monitoring, counseling, and education of his illness. He was very engaging with staff and was aware he required medication to remain stable and ingested the medication without reservation.

During Dave's time in the hospital, CPS returned to the house and discussed the situation with Sonya. Sonya described it to me as, "They came in and told me if I didn't file a restraining order on Dave, I'd never see Jill again. I didn't want to, but they kept telling me he was a danger to me and Jill. I didn't want to sign, I know he wouldn't hurt me or Jill, but they threatened to keep Jill forever and called me a bad mother. I had no choice. I had to get Jill back, so I signed the papers they handed me." The papers were a permanent restraining order filed with the state preventing Dave from seeing his wife and daughter ever again.

When the court notified Dave he was banned from the house; he was devastated. He would no longer be able to see his girlfriend/common-law wife or daughter and was now homeless. He requested supervised visits. CPS declined due to his "violent" nature and threats to staff. It was a difficult situation. Dave moved into a tent close to his family.

After ten months in mental health treatment, Dave asked if the center could act on his behalf. This is when I first met Dave and Sonya and learned of their situation. I contacted Child Protective Services with a release of information from both Sonya and Dave, but CPS refused to discuss the case and recommended that we work on helping Dave separate from his family instead of reconnecting them. I couldn't understand what the issue was; here was a man trying to reconnect with his family, willing to do whatever was asked including supervised visits, having us watch him take his meds every day, active in treatment, etc., but not being able to change CPS opinion of him and the situation.

We filed for a hearing on Dave's behalf to discuss what he would be willing to do to stay with the family. He replied, "anything they ask." I continued to contact Child Protective Services with no progress. Sometimes they would return calls, most of the time they didn't.

During one conversation I was told specifically by the CPS agent, "drop it, it's not going to happen."

The morning of the court hearing I felt confident and a little nervous. I believed the court would listen to the evidence I presented. I was expecting that when the court understood that Dave was stable on his medications, working on treatment, paying child support, the court would hopefully allow him to move back in with his girlfriend and child. I was wrong, very wrong. I don't think I could have been any more wrong and naive about the process and how court was going to play out. I overestimated the belief that reintegration would be fast and sudden. These were serious people who were focused on Dave never seeing his child again. The best I could have hoped for was a step by step reintegration into the house, supervised visits and maybe moving in a year or so. But this was not to be the case.

I went to the courthouse with a coworker of mine. After several minutes, the co-worker ran into a friend of his from college (Jim), the three of us began talking. It turned out Jim was a CPS agent there to attend court. I thought to talk before a court hearing was somewhat unusual, but I said, "difficult case huh." He said, "It's going to be interesting." then the topic changed to family, college, etc., just small talk until we were called in for the hearing.

We went into the courtroom. Dave couldn't afford to hire a lawyer. Dave was on Social Security and was giving most of it to his wife for rent and food. However, Child Protective Services had a lawyer and a damn good one too. She asked several questions about Dave's history. I gave concise and decisive answers. Then she asked, "Have you talked to CPS about the case?" I replied, "Yes." The air sucked out of the room, the entire audience gasped and began to mumble to themselves. I was looking around in bewilderment at the gallery's reaction. I thought to myself, "What did I say?" She looked at me and asked, "Are you sure?" I said, "In the hallway." The mumbling became even louder. She said, "Just a minute your honor" and went to the bench where the CPS agents were sitting and talked. After 30 seconds, she came back and asked, "Did you discuss the merits of the case with any CPS agent." I said, "Oh, that's what you meant. No. We talked Jim the hall, but it was only small talk."

I tend to be a literal person when anxious, and I was extremely worried at this point. We had talked in the hallway, and the case was brought up, but the way she phrased it made it clear. It was the merits of the case she meant. I felt like an idiot. The next question ultimately sank the case, as if we weren't already dead in the water from my last mistake. "Can you guarantee the plaintiff will remain stable?" she asked. I knew he was stable and was managed well on his medications; however, there is no way to guarantee anybody's behavior. Stress, diet, work, sleep can all disrupt a person with mental illness, as can brain chemistry changes from time to time which can cause symptoms to reappear. I sheepishly said, "no." The lawyer asked the judge, "since we can't determine whether or the plaintiffs' behaviors have permanently changed, I request we revisit this case in 1 year." The judge said, "Motion granted, dismissed."

We walked into to the courtyard, where I apologized to Dave, "I am so sorry, I messed up in there." He was sad but calm, "That's ok, you tried, which is more than anyone has done for me since this started." I felt a little better, but I still hurt from the beating I had just received. I kept asking myself, "What the hell happened?", "How did I do so badly?" "What would have worked to get this family back together?" It took me years of long nights berating myself for the mistakes in that courtroom until I figured out the answers.

3. LAWYER UP.

There were several things we did wrong, completely wrong. First, no matter how much it costs, you need to have a lawyer defend you in court. The problem with my answers were question clarity and court procedures. I didn't know where she was leading, and I didn't know what evidence she wanted. A lawyer can redirect the questions so that the information can be presented in a way to assist the defendant in obtaining a fair hearing.

None of the clinical information I prepared was admitted to the court. This is because nobody asked any questions regarding treatment. The CPS lawyer didn't want to know how stable Dave was. She just wanted his diagnosis, and whether he would ever be "cured." She didn't care that he was stable and actively seeking treatment, and it was never brought up. She never asked about how much he was paying his social security check to his family. The CPS lawyer didn't care, and so, it was never brought up. When she asked to "guarantee his stability." My answer could have been followed up with current stability, duration of stability, therapy and daily medication management. Without having a lawyer to represent him, no information on Dave's side was able to be admitted during the proceedings. Without the judge hearing both sides, nothing in Dave's case was going to change, and it wasn't a fair proceeding.

Dave did have the right to cross-examine me and my testimony. He could have asked for clarification as well as the beginning of family reintegration, but he didn't. Why not? He didn't know how or when to. Just like most people, we thought there would be cues to when to speak, present your side, or the judge would suggest cross-examination. In court, there are no cues to when to ask, when to object, or when to motion the judge for actions. And in this case, it destroyed Dave's chances of reintegration with his family. Courts usually will not move on its own for either side, as any action taken has to be requested, then accepted or objected by the other party, then ruled on by the judge. If you don't know when to ask, none of this will occur, and you will lose. You need a lawyer, even a bad one so that the process can be fair.

We all hear about our rights on TV shows like "Law and Order" and think we are innocent until proven guilty. We enter court thinking to ourselves "CPS is going to have to prove that I am a bad parent." We believe when we get into court the judge will hear both sides and know I'm a good parent, or at least not have any evidence of being a bad parent. The judge has to side with me because there is no proof regarding CPS' accusations. This thought process is Wrong. In family court, the requirements for evidence to establish guilt is so low that when CPS brings charges, they need such little evidence, if any at all, for the judge to side with them. I call it, "guilty until proven so." Unlike the standard in criminal court "Innocent until proven guilty." Family court judges use CPS reports as direct evidence in all cases. The rights and care of the child are supposed to be the defining factor of guilt of innocence. But in Family Court your rights as a parent mean nothing. By this standard, the judge will usually take CPS opinion and recommendations for care as proof because CPS is considered the expert regarding child welfare.

The problem with CPS and Family Court is systemic. Child Protective Services is the agency which brings charges. The judge uses those CPS' reports as the evidence of the case. Then the judge decides whether or not to approve CPS' interventions. It would be as if the police charged you with murder; then the judge based his decision completely on the opinion of the officer. The officer could say anything connecting you to the crime, even to the slightest degree (he was in the area at the time), and you have to prove you didn't do it. Most of the lawyers I've worked with don't understand this concept and end up losing CPS cases due to it.

Tip #1, Answer only what you have to.

At the beginning of a case, CPS will receive notification of concerns from someone. Anyone, from anywhere, can report about anything.

When a CPS agent shows up at the door, most people are very stunned. Everyone with children should have a plan in place in case this happens, even though they are a good parent. Just like the police, Child Protective Services is not there to help you. They are there to gather as much information as they can, then to directly use it against you. The main difference between CPS and the police is, you can not invoke your 5th Amendment right to remain silent to protect yourself against Child Protective Services. You have to talk with them. Unlike police who can go back to the office and say, "unable to acquire enough evidence of a crime.", CPS is not allowed to drop the investigation until they get the information they need. They cant return to the office and say, "I didn't get the information." Imagine if they went to a house where they received a report of starving kids, CPS couldn't allow the investigation to be stopped by a parent stonewalling, in fact, they will use refusing to participate in the investigation against you in court.

Since you must speak with CPS, go outside to meet them. Do not invite them inside your home unless it is absolutely necessary. Close the door behind you, lock it and ask, "Why are you here?"

They will come back with, "We have a report of XYZ, and we just need to check up on it." They may ask a question at this point like, "Can we see the child?" or "May we go inside to talk?", the answer to this question should always be another question from you, "What are the charges?" This is very important. You can not defend yourself against the accusations if you do not know what they are. You must be brave and stand your ground. They will continue to ask questions. As difficult as it is (because it is rude to answer a question with a question). Always put them on the defensive by asking questions. Some easy questions to remember are, "What does that have to do with the charges?" and "I don't understand the relevance, can you please explain it to me?" Remember, the more they're talking, the less information they are receiving. If you feel comfortable, normalize the situation. Focus the conversation only on the accusations and explain them away as brief as possible.

Do not volunteer any information, even if you think it is going to be helpful in your case. This is not the time to open up your past and discuss your issues. People like to use personal historical information to support their position to address CPS accusations.

This is a bad idea. When answering a CPS question, make the answers short and sweet with NO BACKSTORY. An example of this would be when CPS says, "We have a report of drug use in the house." The incorrect answer is, "I haven't used drugs in 5 years, I went to rehab and have been clean and sober since". This answer just provided the CPS agent with information that will now be used to build a drug case against you. What is to say you haven't gone back to using? Child Protective Services will use this as, "parent has a history of drug abuse" and could be trying to deceive us. The CPS agent will use any loose end like this as a way to manipulate you and turn your story against you. The only correct answer to this statement is, "No, I don't use drugs." With this statement, it leaves nothing for them to build a case. Nothing that they could use as an "in" to your situation. In the report, the CPS agent will state "suspect denies drug use." Every statement stated to CPS must be thought of in this way. Do not give them a loose thread to pull or your family will unravel like a cheap sweater.

The charges are going to dictate what steps to take next. Depending on the severity of the charges, this will dictate what you can and should do. If the allegations include direct harm to a child (assault, neglect), you will have to let them see the child. This does not mean you have to allow CPS into your house. Have them meet with the child on the front step briefly and in your presence and be sure to record the discussion. Inform CPS that the meeting is being recorded (I'll discuss this in depth in a future chapter). Do not allow CPS to talk with the child alone, EVER. Child Protective Services will be able to make up evidence they need from the child's testimony, and you will have no defense against it. Children do not testify in court, and the words they use are taken at face value, even though you can explain it, that evidence will be used against you. An example would be if they took the child to the car and asked, "has mommy or daddy ever put something in your behind?" The child will answer "yes." "What was it?" will be the next question, and of course the answer will be "I don't know." Now you are losing your son and facing 15 years in prison because you used a rectal thermometer on a three-year-old and the child couldn't explain you were taking his temperature.

Tip #2 Do not let CPS into your house.

I've said this previously, and it bears mentioning again, do not let CPS into your house. The first thing CPS will do when entering your home is to assess the safety of the house for the children. No house is perfect, and no house is beyond repute. If you have breakfast dishes in your sink, unfolded laundry on the couch, haven't swept, dusted, or even if it is considered too clean, it will be used against you. Everyday items will be regarded as dangerous or a health risk: dishwashing soap left on the counter, a piece of a child's toy on the ground where the kid may pick it up and put it in their mouth, dust, or unsecured computer cables. Everything they see, smell and hear will be used in their report to establish a reason to remove your children. Child Protective Services will infer conclusions from what they see, "air freshener to possibly cover the smell of marijuana" or "beer in the refrigerator, possible alcoholic" "unhealthy amount of dust for a child living with asthma" or "not enough sunlight in the home" etc. Numerous possibilities can and will be used against you if you allow them into your house. The amount of risk is limited only by the imagination of the CPS agent, not the actual risk to a child.

If they ask to enter your house, let them know that you are not comfortable having them enter your house. They will ask why, as they investigate for information to use against you. Just let them know you do not trust them and you do not know who they are. I know it sounds bad, but you have to come up with an excuse that they can't use against you. Saying, "I don't want you to" or "it's not clean" gives them another thread to pull. Asking, "Why do you want to go in, what are you looking for?" places the focus back on them. If they insist on entering your home, you will have to invoke your 4th amendment right of (no unreasonable search and seizure). It won't stop them from going in, but it lets them know your rights and willing to fight in court for them.

Although your 4th Amendment right (no unreasonable search and seizure) should prevent CPS and the police from entering your home without a court order, it doesn't. Child Protective Services isn't under the same legal jurisdiction as police. Child Protective Services is not constrained by the police rules of conduct, and the evidence obtained from an illegal CPS search will not automatically be disqualified by obtaining evidence illegally (fruit of the poisonous tree). This is a very touchy subject and should be understood carefully. Child Protective Services are not allowed in your house without an invitation, but if they walk in and conduct the search without a warrant, the family court judge will take the evidence and suggest the parent file charges in criminal court. As well, thirty-three States in America have "Occupational Immunity" which covers the CPS agent in case of illegal actions performed while in the performance of their duties. Which means you may not be able to file a civil or criminal grievance, depending on where you live.

Also, a CPS agent who is willing to go to the judge to get a search warrant for your house will most likely use the same information to obtain an emergency removal order from the same judge. It doesn't take much to get a court order. The CPS agent tells a judge, "we have a report of abuse, and the guardian will not allow us to check on the safety of the child." Child Protective Services, now with a police escort and a warrant is in your house, and the child is in foster care. Your actions depend partially on the charges presented to you while you're talking to CPS. If it's a severe charge, similar to assault or neglect, they will have to see the child to ease their concerns. You may have no other choice but allow them into the house to appease the CPS agent. You may have no choice but to let them in, and if you do, expect a long court trial.

Tip #3 Record all contact with CPS.

Today everyone has some video or audio recording system on their cell phone or in their house. These are a mainstay of today's lifestyle. If you come into contact with CPS, use your camera. Record everything they say and record every visit. Some CPS agents will order you to turn off the recording. However, you are not obligated to do so. To the best of my understanding, public employees do not have the right to privacy while on the job. You have the right to video anyone in your home. They may complain saying, "it's illegal because of wiretapping laws in your state." This statement is also incorrect. Wiretapping involves recording people without their knowledge. By CPS staying for the visit and openly knowing about the recording; they are accepting that they are being monitored. CPS may state that they can not do their jobs because recording violates child confidentiality laws. Since you are the parent, ask to sign a release of information for the person, and this argument goes away. I've personally been told this one several times, "You cannot be here at the meeting for confidentiality issues." I asked the parent "Do you want me here?" When she replied, "yes." I asked for a release of information, and we sat down for a meeting. Isolation is a scare tactic used against the parent from his or her support group and allows CPS to threaten without consequence. Don't let them do this. Confidentiality is placed upon CPS, not you. You have the right to express and explain anything you feel to anybody you want, including friends, family or the media.

I never recommend videoing anyone without their consent. It is just a bad strategy, both for court and during the process. If you record someone with the idea that you are going to catch them in a "gotcha" moment where the CPS agent gets caught in a lie, it will give you 5 minutes of happiness while you watch your children being adopted out to another family. Gotcha moments do not win cases. They provide drama for television shows like Law and Order or CSI. The information can embarrass the CPS agent, but it won't change the dynamic in court at all, even if the evidence is allowed to be presented in the first place.

When recording Child Protective Services, you want all parties to be fully aware they are being recorded. Let them see the recording device. Record them protesting being recorded and your explanation as to why you are recording. Your explanations can include things such as avoiding misunderstandings, being able to replay what was said due to bad memory, or not knowing the background of the CPS agent and wanting to make sure you are safe. Almost any excuse will do. It is imperative to let them see you recording because it changes the CPS agent's demeanor.

Child Protective Services will lie, manipulate, and threaten to get you to surrender to their demands. They do this as a matter of course. They will say things like, "if you don't get that doctor's report to me by Wednesday, I will come back with a court order and the police." This threat is unobtainable and is an empty threat. The CPS agent knows he/she can not remove the child because a report was late. However, if no one is recording, it can be said to strike fear into you, and manipulate you into working with them against your best interests. By recording openly, it forces CPS to choose their words carefully. Using empty threats for meaningless items like a doctor's report would look bad in court and could be used to show the aggressive nature of the CPS agent. By controlling the CPS agent in this way, you can make the discussion feel less hostile for you while limiting how much damaging information the CPS agent can obtain on you. Child Protective Services will use techniques to anger, frustrate and confuse you without the video, then write down your reactions in their report as a personality trait. For example, "Suspect shows hostility towards the conversation, slammed glass onto table showing aggression and predilection to violence." However, with the video watching their every move, the CPS agent knows a statement like this will be contradicted in court by the video and would not support their claim. Worse for them, the discrepancy between CPS report and the recording can undermine the agent's character in court, making them seem dishonest and an unreliable witness.

Tip #4 Be cordial.

Having your children removed by CPS, or being threatened to have your children removed is an emotional situation. I can't think of a worse thing to do to a parent than to take the kids they love and forcefully adopt them out to strangers, just because an anonymous tip from someone you may or may not know caught the ear of a CPS agent and they decided to come for an investigation. The Italian Mafia has rules against targeting children, but our government does not.

Child Protective Services understand this will be a stressful time for you and will use it to their advantage. They will document everything you say, everything you do and fully use it against you in court. Take warning of Dave and Sonya's case, do not threaten violence or harm on the CPS agent. Do not convey hostility or aggression towards them. Talk in a calm, civil tone, with no swearing. This topic is as important as recording them and not allowing them into your house. Your demeanor is the data CPS obtains from you at every meeting you have with them. If you threaten to harm or commit violence against anyone in front of a CPS agent, the CPS agent will perform an emergency removal of your child, and place a restraint order upon you. Then, expect those words to be used against you in not only CPS cases, but as evidence against you in any state or federal case in the future. Ten years down the line you will be considered a threat, even if you have been to counseling, taking medications, apologized, or died. It will be in your state CPS record forever.

CPS documents every action. If you come across to them as reasonable and understanding of the situation, you can manage your way out of CPS charges, as detailed in the next scenario (Frank and his daughter). But if you automatically swear at, threaten CPS, and slam the door in the CPS agent's face, expect police and a court order for search seizure and removal of the child within 30 minutes.

Your presentation is crucial. How you say things and how your body language is in the first few minutes of contact is paramount to your success in defeating the investigation. If you come across as defensive, the CPS agent is automatically going to be suspicious of you. Getting angry and asking over and over, "Why are you here?" and "Who sent you?" will only make a great YouTube video. What doesn't make for great YouTube video's is the long fight with CPS and the expensive court battle that is set against you, which could have been avoided with a different approach.

Your approach should be calm and pleasant as if this an ordinary everyday occurrence. Listening to what's being said and providing short and to the point direct answers can avoid a long, expensive fight later. Don't give CPS any reason to return. "Please and thank you" go a long way to saving thousands of dollars in court costs and your children's future.

Many of the cases in family court do not need to be there. If you know how to handle yourself and the CPS agent, you could be out of trouble before a case is formed. Knowing how and what CPS does, helps in managing these issues. The experience of someone close to me illustrates how handling the investigating agent calmly can work in your favor.

Frank and his daughter.

Frank had just received custody of his fourteen-year-old daughter (Betty), due to Frank's ex-girlfriend (Betty's mother, Janice) passing away. Custody of the Betty was already in the process of changing from Janice to Frank due to Janice's irrational behavior and drug use. The Janice's mother (Shirley) wanted custody but had no way to show Frank was an unfit parent. Frank thought everything was fine until almost a year later when CPS showed up on the doorstep.

Betty, who initially was wanting to live with the Frank, didn't like the rules of the household, as basic as completing homework and phone limitations. Betty complained to Shirley regularly regarding how bad it was to live there. Betty complained about homework, no free time, no friends, etc. Shirley decided the best way to get custody of Betty would be to get Child Protective Services to intervene on her behalf and deem Frank as an unfit father. So Shirley and Betty developed a plan to contact CPS at every opportunity they could, building a record of abuse so that Betty would be removed from Franks home and relocated to Shirley's house.

Betty had regular medical check-up's and had recently seen the doctor three months prior, but it was February, and a severe cold was going around. Betty ended up catching a cold, then went to Frank asking to see a doctor. Frank explained, "No need, it's just a cold. It'll go away in a few days, and if it doesn't get better in a week, then we'll go." Well, when Shirley heard this, she set up an appointment for the doctor for that day, without telling Frank, though she knew Frank planned to take Betty to the doctor if the cold didn't resolve itself in the next few days. Child Protective Services was contacted either by the Shirley or physician per Shirley's request.

When Child Protective Services arrived at the house, Frank was shocked to find out a complaint was filed against him for medical neglect. Frank, who was known for his temper and foul mouth, was able to keep himself together while the CPS agent asked him questions. During the questioning, it became apparent to Frank who contacted CPS and why. The agent asked, "Did you refuse to take your daughter to the doctor when she was sick?" Thinking quickly Frank replied, "She has a cold. Do you take your child to the doctor every time they get the sniffles?" The CPS agent also asked, "When was the last time she saw a physician?" Frank replied, "Three months ago. I can find a receipt if you want to wait a while?" After some discussion of the illness and charges, Frank changed subject to how he came to have custody of his daughter after the ex-girlfriends death and how angry the maternal grandmother was regarding his custody. The charges were deemed unfounded.

Even when charges are considered unfounded, they don't go away. Child Protective Services keeps a record of who calls, who the complaint is about and what the result of the investigation is. Child Protective Services do this to establish a pattern of behavior, either yours or the person reporting. If you get three or four reports from different people, CPS is going to use that to open up an investigation regardless of what was brought in the past. Sometimes it is possible to converse your way out of an investigation, but the investigation report remains on file. Child Protective Services know people use the system as revenge or to obtain custody of children. CPS states they keep these records in to identify people who might abuse the system or are calling to harass others. CPS understands, in many cases the charges are unfounded, but it is up to the CPS agent to determine this based on the interview between the charged and themselves.

Most lawyers agree when talking to the police the less you say the better. The police are looking for information to charge you with a crime. Child Protective Services is looking for information, not to identify a crime, but to substantiate or refute the accusation. There is a big difference between talking to police and talking to Child Protective Services. With police, you have the right to remain silent, and it can not be used against you. This is not the case with CPS. The worst thing you can do with CPS is to refuse to meet with them and ignore the charges. If you refuse to cooperate with CPS and refuse to attend, it will be written in the report. Then the refusal will be used against you and worse, have your child removed from the house. CPS will use any refusal to participate as evidence against you. The judge, always siding on the safety and welfare of the child, (and CPS) will automatically infer that you are hiding something until you prove otherwise. Remember, unlike criminal charges, your right to remain silent is not guaranteed when dealing with CPS.

Consider this hypothetical situation: A CPS agent receives a report of a child being physically beaten. The CPS agent goes to the house and attempts to discuss the accusations with the parents, in an attempt to assess if intervention is warranted. When they talk to the mother, the mother responds with verbal abuse "Go away, you have no right, I don't care who you are." and slams the door in their face. What should CPS do? Ignore the complaint? Walk away and say, "Well, we tried."? How about run away because the parent scared them? No, of course not. They are going to call the police to assist in the interview and assess the parents and the child, and probably remove the child to make sure the child is safe while the initial investigation continues. It only takes one phone call to the central office, and a judge will sign a temporary placement order, contact the police, and the child is removed. Why? Because instead of talking to the CPS agent in a calm voice, the parent decided to yell and scream resulting in losing her child.

As in Tip #4 and described in Dave and Sonya's story, threatening the CPS agent is the worst thing you could do. Not only does it give them a valid reason to contact the police, and judge to remove the child, but it also angers them, making it personal. Threatening a CPS agent is akin to saying, "take my child, please." In mental health, the criteria to hospitalize people is based on three points: danger to self, danger to others, and the inability to care for one's self. Child Protective Services uses similar guidelines in assessing whether a child is to be removed from the house. Opening the door and saying, "Get out of here or there will be trouble!" This behavior shows a parent who is possibly unstable and dangerous. The hostility of a parent provides an opportunity for CPS to remove the child for safety reasons. The second reason is angering them. CPS agents often assess the living conditions and safety of the child. as my dad used to say, "You catch more flies with honey than with vinegar." Being pleasant is the most effective approach. If the CPS agent is undecided regarding whether to remove the child or not, having a friendly, calm voice, and a polite demeanor goes a long way to keep the child home. While an angry CPS agent may go out of their way to find any reason to remove the child. As for apologies, they tend to considered self-serving and are usually too late.

When you talk to the CPS agent, discuss only the charges. See if you can figure out who contacted them and why they did so. If there is any concern, try to normalize the behavior. Just like Frank, you don't take your kid to the doctor every time they get the sniffles. By behaving normal and, explaining the circumstances around it, you look less like an abuser and more like a regular parent doing their best for their child. Look for information. Interviews are not one-sided discussions. Feel free to ask questions of the CPS agent. Ask who filed the charges. Child Protective Service is not legally allowed to tell you, but sometimes they make mistakes or give hints about who filed the charges. Sometimes you can read their body language to receive clues of its a family member, neighbor, teacher or enemy. Ask what the accusations are. Information is vital because you can only defend yourself against what you know. Ask for specifics on how or what they believe happened, and why that is a problem. For example: if someone claimed you hit your child, ask "With what?" How hard were they hit? Where on the body were they struck? Could it have been someone else? Then discuss how it wasn't you and who else it could be.

Sometimes CPS will ignore all evidence and proceed with filing charges with the family court without evidence. In the next story (Mark and Terry), CPS opened and filed a case against a mother with only their opinion as proof, despite having massive amounts of evidence contrary to the charges and CPS' position.

4. Mark and Terry.

Mark and Terry were dating and considering marriage when Terry became pregnant with Jordan. During the pregnancy, the relationship grew strained and eventually ended. Jordan was born a few months later, and that's when the trouble began. Jordan had allergies to milk and wasn't developing correctly. His weight kept fluctuating, and he would vomit, get gassy and have diarrhea if he was given dairy and eggs or anything with dairy or eggs in them. Jordan drank soy milk, which relieved the problem until he began eating solid foods. Terry took him to several specialists to identify what was going on with him. No doctor would be definitive about the cause of Jordan's illness or what to do about it. Due to Jordan's age, it was difficult to determine allergies by standard testing. Terry and Jordan were on the Women, Infant, and Children food program (WIC) for educational support, food, and weight management. Terry tried everything she could. The only thing that worked was to place Jordan on a dietary restriction of no dairy or egg products. Eventually, the symptoms subsided. Jordan was gaining weight, but because of his allergies to milk, he wasn't developing at a typical rate. During this time the Terry was Jordan's sole custodian. However, she maintained an open door policy with her ex-boyfriend and his parents, where they could drop by and visit anytime they wished. Terry was trying to keep all of Jordan's family in contact with him.

A little over a year it was discussed between Terry and Mark for Mark to have partial custody of Jordan. Jordan's grandparents were thrilled. Although, Mark wasn't happy about having more responsibility. Mark wasn't connecting with Jordan, and perhaps he was too young to connect emotionally with his son. Jordan's grandparents wanted to see Jordan as often as possible, and since Mark was living in his parent's basement, so he didn't have much choice.

At this point, Mark would see Jordan with under supervised conditions. Mark would see Jordan only with his parents or Terry in the room. Mark's apartment was deemed unsafe, so he was having his visits at Terry's house, or in Mark's parent's part of the home.

One day he came into Terry's house in a particularly bad mood. At this time, he pushed Terry, throwing her off balance. Mark then went to Jordan and yanked the blanket from underneath him, causing Jordan to tumble over uncontrollably. The police were contacted, and Mark was charged with assault and criminal mischief. Later, Mark was found guilty of these charges, placed on a six-month probation and released from custody. Child Protective Services investigated and found no reason to pursue charges against Mark. The police and court considered the situation criminal, but CPS decided it didn't warrant an investigation.

During some visits, Mark would have supervised visits at Jordan's grandparent's house. When Jordan would return to Terry's home from Mark's house, Terry would find blotching on Jordan's skin, rashes, and he would wheeze when he cried. Terry would question Mark about it, but her inquiries would usually go ignored. Terry, being allergic to dogs herself, decided to check with Mark about their family pet. It seemed that Jordan had inherited a dog allergy from his mother. After getting a refusal from Mark to alleviate the problem, Terry discussed the issue with Jordan's pediatrician and allergist. After a consult between doctors, both agreed on allergy medications to remedy the symptoms. The medicines made Jordan sleepy and disturbed his sleep and feeding schedule, but since Mark refused to remove the dog, it was Terry's only option to help her son.

Mark and his Jordan's grandparents knew about Jordan's allergies. They were aware of the difficulties Jordan had with dairy and eggs but decided to have pizza for dinner anyway. They chose to ignore the fact Jordan had a problem with certain foods. This was a bad mistake. About an hour after eating pizza, Jordan began vomiting and had diarrhea. It was so severe Jordan's grandparents decided to take Jordan to the emergency room. While there, Jordan's grandparents told the doctor they didn't know why he was vomiting. They suggested it could be the medications that Terry was giving Jordan, and stated how often Terry took Jordan to doctor's appointments, "hoping to find something wrong with him." After the symptoms subsided, Child Protective Services was contacted by the Emergency Room doctor, to investigate the claim of medical abuse of a child. Everyone in the medical profession, including ER staff, are mandated to report any possible signs of abuse. Whether they believe there is abuse or not, the ER had to contact CPS or risk losing licensure.

Child Protective Services showed up at Terry's house to discuss the ER visit. Terry was very cordial and explained Jordan's the situation to the agent. She showed documents of the WIC food program involvement, allergist reports of egg sensitivity and milk allergies. Terry showed medical records showing Jordan's recent weight gains. Child Protective Services received all the documentation and releases of information for all of Jordan's physicians. Then CPS began the legal process of removing Jordan from Terry's custody "for his medical safety." Because of her demeanor and being cordial, they couldn't prove imminent threat and file for emergency removal.

Terry was beside herself. She was utterly panicked and distraught at the thought of not only having Jordan removed but also of losing all custody and possibly contact with her son forever. Terry tried all the things she could think of to prove he had an allergy, including having the allergist contact CPS. Nothing worked. Child Protective Services drafted a service plan which identifies current problems and how to resolve them. Terry refused to sign the service plan and politely expressed that she was not going to cooperate anymore with the CPS investigation against her. Child Protection Services drew the emergency removal card and played it saying, "If you decide not to let us in and talk to us we WILL remove Jordan, and you will never see him again." That was the exact quote; CPS was not playing around.

Terry decided to write a letter to the governor for assistance. I am adding it to show how distraught Terry was. Here is the full text copied precisely as initially written including errors, except omitting the hospital names to maintain confidentiality:

"I am writing to you on behalf of my one-year-old son Jordan. His father and I are unmarried, and we have joint custody with me having fill placement. Jordan has been diagnosed with asthma and allergies by his pediatrician and a pulmonary specialist. On Sunday, during their visitation, the father and his parents took Jordan to (hospital name omitted) and called DCYF to charge me with overmedicating Jordan. Since time DCYF has talked to the doctors and me to justify the medications. Jordan receives precisely what the doctor prescribes. To my surprise, DCYF asked me to take Jordan to a safe clinic on Friday, Sept 3rd. At the clinic hostilely questioned by a doctor about visitation about me trying to keep Jordan away from his father, about destroying Jordan's relationship with his father and did not test for drugs or had Jordan's doctor records. I was very confused by the line of questioning and was told to remove Jordan from asthma medications which protect him. That I had no legal right to a second opinion and that the father and grandparents were going to expose him to a dog without medication and without medical personnel anywhere they want to.

Why is it that DCYF after looking at him for 5 minutes has the right to make decisions when other doctors have been involved with his care. I need immediate help in this matter because my son's life could be in danger. I cannot believe a government agency whose job it is to protect children could order this.

I would appreciate their help in this matter. Why can I not get a second opinion and why is DCYF's opinion higher than any other doctor's opinion. If question of overmedicating why was there no testing done to find out when he was taken to (hospital omitted) or at the safe clinic.

I have no problem with Jordan seeing his father, but I don't want his life to be in danger. DCYF told me not to take Jordan to the emergency room that because if I took him and the father did not, agree it would be my negligence."

Terry is a family friend. Knowing my professional background, she asked if I could help her. I said, "I'll do what I can, but it looks like they're out to get you for something. I don't know what, but something's not right." I asked Terry if it was ok for me to sit in on a meeting with her and CPS. She agreed, and I was in attendance at the next meeting.

I sat on one end of the couch when the doorbell rang. The CPS agent was right on time. I explained to the CPS agent that I was there to help with Terry's understanding of what is going on because her anxiety was not allowing her to comprehend everything being said. The CPS agent protested, "Everything is confidential. It is not allowed for you to sit in the meeting. "I replied, "Ok, then can she video it for her records?" "Absolutely not!!!" commanded the CPS agent. I explained that as a therapist I understand the need for confidentiality and that Terry has asked for me to sit in on the meeting. The CPS agent reluctantly relented, and Terry was required to sign a release of information for my attendance. The meeting went as follows: "Terry, how are you doing?" "Good. Nervous but good", Terry replied quickly then we sat and said nothing to each other for an hour. The tension was so thick you could almost see it. Nothing else was said until the CPS agent looked at her watch, stood up and said, "Ok, I have to go to my next appointment. Same time next week?" Terry replied, "Uh -huh." Terry got up to walk the agent to the door, the CPS agent leaned in and asked very quietly, "Next time it has to be just you and me." Terry said, "Uh, why?" CPS agent still whispering, "Because I need to go over some things with you." Terry, in a brilliant statement, replied, "Oh, don't worry, anything you say to me you can say in front of him. I trust him." Irritated, the CPS agent walked to her car and drove away. The CPS agent never asked to see Jordan, never asked if Jordan was growing, did not check any medical records, and did not ask one word regarding Jordan.

I went to the kitchen to discuss things with Terry, "That was the weirdest, most awkward meeting I have ever had....and I work with schizophrenics who don't respond to heavy drugs, so that's saying something." We both laughed as my joke cleared the tension from the room. Terry said, "She doesn't want you back." I asked, "Why do you think that?" She said, "She asked for you not to be here next time." I answered, "Good luck with that, I'll be here as long as you allow me. But it's interesting. She doesn't want anyone else to hear what is being said in the meetings. No recordings and no record except what she's writing down." Terry asked, "Yeah, why is that?" I answered, "Because she wants to threaten you, push your buttons, and make you react so that she can make you out to be the bad guy in all of this. With me there, she can't because it would go against her in court, but without me, it's her word against yours, and she's the professional. But for the life of me, I don't know why she has this agenda. Did you do anything to piss them off?" Terry replied, "Not that I can think of." I asked, "Can I see your service plan? Let's see what they want to work on with you." As I was looking over the document, it hit me, like a ton of bricks. Right there, in bold black letters, "Medical abuse, rule out Munchausen's syndrome by proxy." My jaw dropped, I couldn't believe what I was reading. For those who don't know "Munchausen's syndrome by proxy " is a condition where a mother will deliberately poison or injure a child to seek attention from medical professionals and family members. It was portrayed in the movie "The Sixth Sense" in which a child was deliberately poisoned by the mother until the child succumbed to the poison. Munchhausen's syndrome by proxy is exceptionally rare, even the most liberal statistics rate it as high as 1000 in 2,500,000 parents that can be classified having this disorder. In this case, Child Protective Services was accusing that Terry was making

Jordan sick by claiming allergies and taking him for unnecessary tests and medications.

The service plan had twelve points. Terry was to: contact the physician if Jordan was ill, give meds only prescribed by a doctor, meet with a nutritionist, keep a journal of Jordan's food intake, be available for CPS home visits, have a milk challenge to determine the presence or absence of a milk allergy, follow recommendations of the milk challenge, work with Early Intervention Services and follow their recommendations, sign all releases, follow up with CPS referrals. None of these things were discussed in the meeting, as there was no conversation to be had. Terry was actively following most of the items in the service plan before CPS intervention. Terry had previously discussed conducting a milk challenge with the pediatrician, allergist, and gastroenterologist. All of the doctors stated it was either unnecessary or unsafe. Child Protective Services over-ruled their judgments and required a milk challenge at a local hospital.

I began to realize this was an unusual case. There was something underhanded going on. It was apparent that Jordan had allergies and sensitivities to food. The documentation stated that testing was either positive or inconclusive due to age. Three different doctors including a pediatric allergist, pediatric gastroenterologist, and Jordan's primary pediatrician corroborated on the diagnosis and treatment yet Child Protective Services still wanted to relocate Jordan to his father's care due to Terry's medical neglect or Munchausen's syndrome by proxy. As I continued to read, nothing in the CPS plan related to the treatment of Terry, care of Jordan, or maintaining the family. What I read was shocking, "will have child hospitalized and observed for 48 hours, no medical visits or medication changes, all medications will be reviewed and counted at weekly meetings, etc." Terry's mental health was not being addressed, nothing regarding resolution. The only topics considered were ones CPS could obtain evidence against Terry. After reading the service plan, I looked at Terry and said, "No, you're not paranoid, they are out to get you."

Terry couldn't understand. She wasn't doing this for attention, so why would CPS think she was? We began discussing a plan for her defense. If we did nothing, CPS was going to revoke her parental rights and remove Jordan from her life.

The first thing we did was to contact all three of the physicians and have them write letters stating that the care Jordan had received was in their opinion due to an allergy/organic medical condition rather than it being caused by the parent. All of the physicians agreed to help. Secondly, we set up an appointment with a forensic psychologist for a baseline non-biased psychological evaluation of Terry. The psychologist would run tests to see if there was any underlying truth to claims of attention seeking behavior. Thirdly, we set up a chart to track any time when Jordan got sick. Tracking Jordan's illnesses revealed a pattern. There was a connection between increased symptoms and visits with Mark. The chart showed that whenever he came home from his father's home/Mark's mother's home, Jordan would have stomach pains, vomiting, diarrhea, rashes and wheezing. We thought it might be helpful to show CPS that it was the visits with Mark causing the symptoms.

Our next weekly appointment with CPS didn't go much better than the first. The CPS agent was polite and friendly, but she didn't talk much, didn't ask anything about Jordan, didn't ask to see him, didn't count the meds in the medicine bottles, didn't ask about mental health counseling. The only discussion regarding the plan was: "Did you read the service plan? Do you understand it? Will you sign it for me?" Terry replied, "I understand it, but I don't agree with it, so I'm not going to sign it." The CPS agent responded with a light threat, "You know if you don't sign it, we will take you to court." Terry said, "I know, we are going there anyway. I don't hold you personally responsible, you're a very nice person, but I don't agree with what is written, so I can't sign it."

All of the meetings went similarly. CPS, "Want to sign?" Terry, "Nope." Terry and I discussed the service plan. By signing the plan, CPS would use it in court as a sign that Terry agreed with CPS and would use it to take Jordan away. It would be tantamount to a confession in criminal court, once you confess it is over. Do not sign anything CPS gives you unless you and your attorney agree. If they force your signature by a court order that is fine, but I recommend never to sign anything other than a release of information. Admission of guilt removes your ability to fight in court, but of course, listen to your attorney, and discuss your options with them.

Terry went to her forensic psychology appointment for testing and evaluation. The testing took over three hours. Terry was interviewed, given several paper and pencil tests, discussed the reasons behind needing the evaluation and observation. When Terry received the results she was diagnosed with 'mild to moderate anxiety due to situational factors in her life'; no evidence of attention seeking, personality disorders or Munchausen syndrome by proxy. The rest of the document reflected which tests were used and how the psychologist determined the diagnosis. We were relieved at the results, but not surprised.

Next, there were letters from Jordan's doctors. This came as a shock. For some reason, almost all of the doctors we requested letters from changed their minds about submitting their medical opinions. The allergy doctor would only see Jordan sporadically; the endocrinologist refused to see Jordan anymore. Jordan's primary care physician, who had provided a short but direct statement for Terry, had immediately retired. Completely out of the blue and without notification of his patients, he closed his practice and retired. I was amazed. How could it be that all of them changed their minds so quickly knowing the family as well as they do? Discussing it with

Jordan's pediatrician, Terry asked, "Are you closed because CPS threatened you?" The doctor, wanting to help replied, "I can't say no to that." Then it became painfully obvious; CPS contacted all of the doctors Jordan was seeing and influenced them not to intercede on Terry's behalf. I don't know what they said to each doctor, but whatever it was, it made them all stop medical care of Jordan. I'm not sure if any legal wrongdoing occurred, but I know it was unethical to interfere with the medical treatment of a small child. But without anybody willing to talk to us, that avenue of recourse was unavailable.

Child Protective Services continued to pressure Terry. They were demanding Terry place Jordan in the hospital for 24-hour observation for the milk challenge. Terry, a Wal-Mart employee, explained that for her to do that was cost prohibitive, CPS would not relent, and eventually was able to convince the hospital to do the observation for their agency. I don't know if CPS paid for the service, or it was a courtesy, but when Terry and Jordan went to the hospital, the hospital staff were unhappy to see her and were indignant to the point of rude. The hospital must have known what the observation was regarding and the hospital staff had no reservations about letting their feelings be known. Child Protective Services explained the observation to us as, "having the nurses watch to see if Jordan has any changes in symptoms during the milk challenge. The hospital was in case Jordan needed medical care." I explained to Terry, "You know this is a trap? Child Protective Services is watching to see whether or not you try anything to hurt Jordan and whether or not you try to socialize with the hospital staff and expect to be video recorded every time you enter the room." Terry was stricken with fear," What do you mean? ", "Why would they do this?" I explained that they weren't looking for his allergies because they weren't changing his diet, that they were giving Terry the opportunity to seek attention from the staff. Terry asked, "What do I do?" I explained, "Nothing. Do nothing. Be with Jordan, be yourself, don't talk too much to the staff about what they are doing and play on your phone. And remember, you are being videoed." According to the report generated by the hospital, "Nothing of interest occurred." The report was filled with data on how much food was eaten, how long he slept, medications given, etc., but when it came to interactions…" minimally involved" "obsessed with smartphone." As a side note, "obsessed with smartphone" isn't a symptom of Munchausen's by Proxy.

Considering the lack of information CPS had, when they called for a meeting, I was expecting that they were going to have a meeting to discuss dropping the charges. We were invited to a meeting to the Child Protective Services central office with Mark, his parents, his lawyer, and the Medical Director of CPS (a licensed MD). The actual medical director of Child Protective System was involved. I began to realize this was much more than just a simple case, and this went to the highest positions of the agency.

The medical director of CPS reports to the director of CPS who reports to the Secretary of Health and Human Services, who reports to the Governor of the state. But why would someone that high up in the agency care so much about a Wal-Mart employee and her son?

Reading the report from the medical director was one contradiction after another. The report stated, "Follow up asthma. Exposed to family members yesterday who have cats and dogs. Seems like an hour later he seems to be wheezing.", "Wheezes on and off possibly with animal exposure" "Dussy (sp) and crying more. Couch with a runny nose. Upper airway congestion, clear drainage from nose."

etc. However, most comments from the medical director downplayed any connection between allergies and Jordan's condition. As the director stated in the report, "I think it is very important to determine whether this child has allergies." Although the CPS director noted "Allergy NOS-995.3 primary" as the main diagnosis, she refused to consider this as a cause of Jordan's physical condition and made the decision it was child neglect and medical abuse. The director stated, "I am concerned that mother is using the "allergy excuse" to limit the child's access to the father." This statement showed the focus of CPS being on the parents' relationship rather than the well-being of the child.

As we were sitting down to the meeting, I asked Terry if she gave the copy of the forensic report to her attorney. She hadn't, but she had brought it with her. The meeting began with a short speech from the medical director. The medical director stated, by review of the medical records she believed Terry suffered from numerous mental health issues relating to her son. Terry used her son for attention seeking behavior and that in her opinion "the child should be under the father's care." The medical director also stated, "I have recently completed a study of Munchhausen Syndrome by Proxy, Terry fits all the criteria as seen in my study." I was sitting in shock as she openly admits to personally overseeing this case and being completely in the corner of Mark, and using her personal research as evidence against Terry. "I have it under a trusted third party who knows the situation well, Jordan would be better off with his father."

While the medical director was giving her speech, I whispered to Terry to pass the report to her attorney. "Tell her to read it and then give it to the doctor (medical director)." After she completed her speech, the medical director asked Mark's attorney, "any thoughts?" Mark's attorney began with discussing the lack of communication between Mark and Terry and how it was negatively influencing his relationship with Jordan. As Mark's attorney was speaking Terry's lawyer passed the psychological report to the medical director. As she read, you could see the confidence drain from her face as the report refuted everything she had just declared in the room. The more the medical director read, the more her face turned red, and you could see the anger in her eyes.

After Mark's attorney spoke, it was Terry's lawyer's turn. She spoke of opening up the channels of communication, referred to numerous e-mails which were ignored by Mark, and both parties being more inclusive in Jordan's life. When she was done, the medical director whispered to Terry's attorney, "Has (Mark's Attorney) seen this?" "Not yet" was her reply. The director changed her tune, suggesting an agreement be made to allow more time to be spent with the father, suggesting joint custody and the father be aware and invited to all medical appointments. As she was saying this, you could see the confusion on the faces of Mark's parents and in Mark's attorney. Mark wasn't paying much attention as he was playing with a pen. This completely took the air of superiority from CPS. Mark's attorney was looking at the director with a puzzled look and said, "we are not averse to these requests" with the director giving an" I'll explain later" look back at him. Terry's lawyer stated, "we will consider the recommendation; however, I should discuss this with my client."

The meeting ended with the standard pleasantries as Terry's lawyer said, "Let's get out of here before we talk." We met back at the lawyer's office. The lawyer asked, "Where did you get that?" Terry replied, "We thought it was the best idea considering they're accusing me of being crazy." The lawyer said, "Well, it took the fight out of them. When did you get that report?" "A couple of weeks ago, sorry for not giving it to you sooner, but I haven't seen you in a while," replied Terry. I asked, "Do either of you know what she (the medical director) meant when she said she knew of this by the third party?" Neither could identify who it could be.

With the meeting out of the way, I was reasonably confident CPS was going to drop the charges and try to repair the damage they caused. This was not to be the case. A court hearing was set up for four weeks ahead, with weekly meetings to continue to discuss signing the CPS service plan. I attended every meeting, which consisted of, "please sign the progress plan, or we'll have to take you to court." Terry continued to refuse, politely but firmly saying, "We are already going to court, what's the difference."

A couple of weeks went by, and I was at every weekly meeting. One week, Terry had a different look on her face. The kind of look an eight-year-old has when they have a secret they are just dying to tell someone. After the meeting she said, "I found it, I figured out who the 3rd party was." I said, "Really, Who?!?!" Terry replied, "Mark's aunt, who is a nurse who worked at a hospital previously with the director." "Mark's mother's sister was a nurse for (the medical director) at a different job and maintained her friendship." I asked, "How did you figure this out?" Terry answered, "I remember Mark mentioning his aunt and being a nurse, put it together and connected them with a Google search."

To me, that was a brilliant piece of detective work. Now we knew what was going on. Mark or one of Mark's parents contacted Mark's aunt to ask the CPS medical director to influence CPS to push for Mark to receive custody of Jordan. The Child Protective Services' medical director was abusing her power, influence, and research as a way to discredit Terry, and remove her parental rights. It was a convoluted plan, but the only one that made any sense. It explained why Child Protective Services wasn't interested in any treatment of Terry, why the CPS agents never asked any questions about Jordan, who the "third party" was, and why CPS was so intent on removing Jordan from Terry to place Jordan with Mark, who never seemed interested in Jordan. It was an "ah-ha" moment, but as with most conspiracy theories, very little proof. We couldn't prove the aunt contacted the CPS medical director. We couldn't prove any wrongdoing at all. Child Protective Services wouldn't talk about anything but the CPS plan being signed. It wouldn't matter anyway unless we could find a direct written paper trail to connect the dots, and besides Terry didn't have the money to sue anyway. It was disappointing, but it was the reality. You need money to sue, and even if you have the evidence, it is a risk most people won't take and Child Protective Services rely on this.

The morning of the court date came, Terry was near panic as her fear of this case was causing dramatic anxiety, as it would anyone. She was terrified of what was going to be done in the hearing. I tried to help settle her anxiety with small talk and some reminders of how well she has done so far, but the constant barrage of CPS threats of "sign or go to court" and "you have to work with us, or we will take Jordan away" was pushing Terry to her limits. Terry had been threatened and intimidated every week for over nine months regarding her son. I don't know many people who can take stress like that without cracking. As we were walking into the hearing, the CPS agent said, "Last chance to sign. Will you sign it, please?" Terry looked at her lawyer, and the Lawyer shrugged, Terry replied, "I guess." I was shaking my head "no," but Terry signed at the bottom.

We went into the courtroom. Mark's attorney began with a change of heart. He asked the court to amend the child custody agreement to "full shared custody" instead of Mark having "sole custody" to "have Mark be invited and allowed at all medical appointments." He also requested to "increase visitation to include Jordan staying over for one week per month to be scheduled by the parents." "No objection" was entered into the record by Terry's lawyer. The judge asked, "Does CPS have anything they want to add?" CPS agent replied, "No, your honor." The judge asked, "Does CPS want to continue with its case?" The CPS agent replied, "No your honor, we will no longer be involved in this case. We are closing the case." The judge, looking irritated, as if she had wasted her time said, "Amending custody agreement for full shared custody, Mr. (Mark) to be allowed increased visitation of one week per month to be worked out between the parties, and Mr. ____ (Mark) to be invited to all doctor appointments....dismissed." And the judge stood up and abruptly walked out.

By all intents and purposes, Terry won. However, as we walked out of court Terry was distraught, "I lost custody of Jordan, I can't believe we lost!" It took a few minutes for the lawyer and me to explain to Terry that she had won the case with a few changes to the custody agreement. After explaining she would still be in physical custody of Jordan and the difference would be that Mark gets more visitation and can sit in on doctor appointments. Most important, Child Protective Services was out of her life and couldn't touch her, or Jordan. That didn't sink in for a few weeks. I would still get phone calls regarding, "Do you think CPS will….?", and my reply would always be, "CPS won't come at you anymore, because you fought them and won."

Terry was very traumatized by the whole thing and suffered classic signs of Post-Traumatic Stress Disorder from the ordeal. She would have nightmares, cold sweats, flashbacks, anger, etc., but in time the symptoms reduced, and she went back to her normal life. The fighting between her and Mark regarding Jordan continued for several years after, but because she fought CPS and won she wasn't letting Mark drive the conversation anymore, and I believe the ordeal made her a stronger person.

Just for the record, as Jordan grew it was determined he was allergic to milk, had an egg sensitivity and is allergic to pet dander, just like Terry explained to the doctors. He also was diagnosed with

ADHD and is an extremely active child. All these conditions explain all the wheezing, coughing, skin blemishes and inconsistent weight gains. The problem was not the mother, who was doing her best in the situation, but a child with unusual needs and irregular symptoms.

Tip #5 Always hire a lawyer.

All cases are different, and each requires its own strategy and tactics to defend against CPS intervention. Always listen to your lawyer in the case, but remember it is your life and your child on the line, so the ultimate decision is yours. No matter what pressure (and you will receive a ton of pressure), from both sides, you must decide the best option for you and your child. In every case that proceeds from initial investigation to open case. You always need a lawyer. Like I mentioned in Dave's case, without a lawyer you won't know the questions to ask; let alone the procedure for getting to ask the questions. You'll have lost before you enter the courtroom, because you'll never get your side of the issue heard. The judge doesn't care about you, not as a person or as a parent. The judge cares about the hearing and the welfare of the child, and in most cases will side on caution which includes CPS involvement in your life.

Even a bad lawyer is better than no lawyer. I wasn't happy with Terry's lawyer. Terry's lawyer was doing the work "pro bono" and seemed not to care about setting up a defense. Everything she did was either directed by Terry or concocted on the spot; I refer back to Terry's psychological evaluation. A good lawyer will set up a plan to defend against CPS, identify ways to discredit the charges and direct Child Protective Services' position toward a more favorable outcome. I believe Mark and Terry's outcome was great for Jordan, but that didn't come from Terry's attorney, it was a compromise when CPS realized they didn't have ground to stand on, and Terry was willing to fight all the way. A good lawyer will take time to understand the case and not just present an opposing viewpoint, but also cite legal precedence to force the court to choose for the defense. No court case is simple but a lawyer who only stands up and says, "no objections" isn't fighting for the benefit of the parent or child.

Lawyers get paid, and you get what you pay for. I said before, "a bad lawyer is better than no lawyer. " Understand, a lawyer that is not getting paid has little stake in the fight. In their minds, the time they spend on your case "pro bono" is considered billable time which they could use to make money somewhere else. It is the way the system is set up. Law is a business like anything else, and the business needs money to run. When choosing a lawyer, more expensive doesn't mean more invested in the case, but in general, the more a lawyer costs, the more they want to work on it. The exception and there are always exceptions, are brand new lawyers straight out of school. New lawyers, who don't have much experience, will fight very hard for less money. New lawyers do this because most are still ideological about "fighting for what's right" and they are getting paid partly with experience. Experience in any field is difficult to obtain. You have to work many years at a big law firm to get the opportunity to present cases, and by letting new lawyers take the case; what they lack in experience they make up with tenacity.

Despite the law stating there is no "specialization" of attorneys and, the attorneys themselves stating they can handle any case brought to them, the truth of the matter is they can't. Nobody could. An attorney who manages divorce and disability claims is allowed to represent the defense in a criminal trial for murder if he or she so chooses, but it is in the best interest of the defendant to obtain an attorney who is a known criminal trial attorney for that case. The skills needed for each specialty are entirely different and will make a less than capable defense in court when the wrong skills are used.

The same with CPS/Family Court. Family court attorneys tend to focus on civil actions, divorce and child placement, alimony payments and contracts. In CPS cases, a special attorney should be hired, because CPS family court isn't Criminal or Family but a hybrid of the two with limited protection of the constitution and no oversight. Family law with CPS cases is an uphill battle from the start. From strong-arm tactics to obtain information and evidence to compulsory requirements (classes, therapy, etc.) Before being found guilty of any charges, CPS will use avoiding these requirements will be used against you as your lack of willingness to cooperate with CPS and a lack of determination to maintain custody of your children. One place to start is www.fightCPS.com. Although I am not affiliated with this website or any of the attorneys listed, I have seen great articles from this website including what to do if CPS is using your own CPS history against you. Do not be afraid to ask questions of the attorney, since he or she works for you, and you need to be sure this is the person who is going to fight the hardest for your child, regardless of where you are in the case. Ask questions about their history with CPS cases, Family vs. Criminal court statutes, how would they begin to defend you and your children, and most self-serving, have they read this book.

A family law defense attorney must have three prime traits; first, they must be willing to listen to your concerns and issues. An attorney who seems distracted during your conversation isn't going to understand the nuances of your case, and they may even be dismissive of your concerns. Never accept, "Don't worry, I'll take care of it" as an answer from your attorney, ask "How are you going to take care of it?" The attorney should be a partner in the defense, not the defense itself. An engaged attorney will discuss the plan of attack, step by step process to expect and how he/she is going to counter each obstacle, CPS is going to provide to the case.

Second, an engaged attorney will be on the attack. The attorney should not sit and wait for CPS to contact him or her but should contact CPS and begin the defense by sending releases of information and obtaining all the documentation CPS has regarding the case. CPS refusal to release the record is illegal, and they know it. CPS does not get paid for paperwork, and it helps drive up costs of the case.

Third, the attorney needs to care about the outcome of the case. Nobody wants to lose, but an attorney who has to win fights harder. The result of the case is about getting CPS out of your life, sometimes negotiation is the best alternative, but sometimes court is necessary and having an attorney who wants to win in either case is going to give you the best chance.

5. Expectations

Fear of reprisal from CPS is a legitimate concern. Remember the doctors from Terry and Mark, the same doctors who agreed to treat and defend Jordan, then refused to write letters, refused to treat Jordan. One retired because of fear of reprisal. If they can do that to doctors in the community with long-standing practices, what can they do to the average person making $40,000 per year? Could Child Protective Services open an investigation on them for intimidation? Could CPS leak information to family, friends, and neighbors that would ruin a reputation? Just saying, "Hello, I'm XYZ from Child Protective Services, I would like to ask you a few questions about your neighbor…" opens up a person's reputation to scrutiny. Even worse, if the questions are leading or emotionally charged, false evidence can be collected to help CPS prove a false case and the neighbor, who just wanted to help a friend, ending up with similar CPS problems as the friend they are trying to help. I'm expecting a knock on my door from CPS after writing this book, just as a form of intimidation.

I can only imagine what CPS said to the doctors who wanted to help Terry. To turn your back on a patient is amazingly cowardly, but I'm assuming the threat was severe. It is the only way I can comprehend a physician retiring from a thriving practice overnight would be if they were threatened with license revocation, or worse abuse charges themselves.

Every case I have been a part of has one similarity, I call it "disappearing supports." It happens in all cases. Everyone has friends and family to some extent. But every time you call on these friends I see the same thing, "sure, I'll write you a letter of recommendation", "sure, I'll go to court with you", "you did nothing wrong, I will do….", but when the time comes to produce a letter, go to court or help in any way everybody runs for the hills. I've asked myself on numerous occasions why people do this. It can be very frustrating when you are trying to help put a case together. But sadly, I think it comes down to fear. Testifying in court isn't easy, especially when your going against the state, let alone having your child at risk for removal based on what is said. Self-doubt creeps into mind, and people fear Child Protective Services retributions. Sadly, don't expect help from friends or neighbors. They know you, they like you, but very seldom will they appear in court to testify on another's behalf. Teachers and most professionals aren't allowed to testify unless under subpoena. There is a legal risk for anybody regarding testifying, and most managers will not allow it. Being on the stand can be nerve-racking and what you say becomes the legal record. That means if a person admits, no matter how inadvertently, to a misdoing, issue, problem or crime, it is now public record and can be used against a person in another case.

Tip #6 Find an advisor you can trust.

Discussing CPS involvement with your family and friends can be embarrassing. To have CPS in your life can make you look and feel like a criminal or even worse, a bad parent. CPS prey on this fear and will sometimes tell people not to discuss the case outside of the people involved. CPS is bound by confidentiality laws, but not the parent or guardian. Discussing the case with a trusted outside source can give insight into what CPS is going after, how to handle yourself, relieve stress and how to gain focus.

The first question on many people's minds when they get contacted by CPS is, "What did I do?" By discussing the issue openly and honestly with a trusted friend, counselor or uninvolved family member, it can open a person's eyes to how they got into this situation and how to get out of the situation. Discussing what was said and documented by CPS can give insights into how CPS plans to attack you and how to defend against it. Every case is different, but by listening to your confidant, you can determine whether the attack has enough merit to cause serious problems, what is needed to refute the charges, how to handle CPS future visits and what it will take to end CPS involvement. Remember, winning isn't only defeating CPS in court. It is getting them out of your life without destroying the family and with as little cost to you as possible.

6. Strategy

Your strategy should begin before the first contact. It should be a plan for if CPS comes to your house. I am fully aware I am on a CPS list somewhere as a problem person, just because I wrote this book. So before I started writing, I planned what I want the first CPS contact to look like and how to manage it. This strategy includes four goals, diffusing the CPS charge (information), proving CPS wrong (data conflicts), keeping CPS out of my life, and maintaining custody of my children (court). Everything I plan to do is based on these four goals. Being right, being belligerent or asserting constitutional rights are nowhere on this list.

In every defense, you need strategy (plan), and tactics (actions). The approach is predicated on the situation you find yourself in, what the charges are, and what you want as an outcome. A strategy is a plan of action to diffuse, redirect and redirect the charges that are presented. A strategy is not, "I'm going to make fools of CPS" or

"I'm going to tell the judge what I think, and she's going to do what I say." These are only wishes and will make you look like a fool in court, and to lose your child.

You may have noticed, in this book I have referred to everything as a defense. That's because everything you do with CPS is a defense. A family court hearing is not the place to attack CPS, it will make you vulnerable and considered "emotionally unstable," and the judge doesn't care. If the CPS agent walked straight into your house, took a beer from your fridge and drank it in front of you, it is irrelevant to your case. That needs to be addressed in a conduct report to CPS superiors, or in a lawsuit for misconduct, but not in family court. Remember, the court cares only about the court proceedings and the welfare of the child. This means crimes perpetrated against you by Child Protective Services' will not be addressed in family court. The focus is on you, not them. You need to show evidence none of the things occurred or show third-party evidence that Child Protective Services is wrong. You are defending yourself, and the mindset should be only of that.

Each line in the CPS service plan must be argued and defended. It is imperative to take each of the items from the progress plan and isolate each one then provide evidence directly countering each charge. Defense isn't just for the main issues, but as many as possible. A good lawyer will be able to present this to the judge. There is a possibility CPS will surrender the case at this point, due to the counter-evidence, however as a defendant do not consider this a probable conclusion. Each item should be listed and some document provided to disprove the issue, this becomes the crux of the defense. It is vital to provide these documents to the court. The records become the witnesses that CPS cannot argue. It is easy to confuse a witness on the stand, it is easy to ignore a parents rights, but documentation becomes a thorn in the side of any prosecution. These documents can be almost anything from grocery receipts, video, to medical reports to psychiatric evaluations to checking account records. Every paper and video proves something that can be used to chip away at the CPS case.

Court cases mostly have four people involved, CPS agent, CPS Lawyer, the Judge and you. This is the way CPS likes it. They can control the hearing if you don't have a lawyer and the scales of justice are balanced 75/25 in their favor, with a lawyer it balances out to 60/40 in their favor. Your strategy must include more than your testimony, or you will lose. Your plan must consist of what you can bring to increase your evidence to at least 51/49 your favor. Unlike criminal court, you must defend yourself. The standard of proof is very low (Preponderance of Evidence) in Family court, "in our professional opinion" is often all that is needed from CPS for the judge to side with them. It does come down to the opinion of the CPS agent at times. It is up to the parent to disprove their suspicions. The CPS physician in Terry's case accused Terry of having Munchausen's by proxy without any actual evidence; only an opinion gleaned from third-party sources. By bringing evidence to light that proves otherwise, CPS finds they have no way to prove their case. What evidence do you have that you are not medically neglectful or physically abusive? What evidence is CPS using to investigate the charges?

7. Tactics

In every defense, you need a strategy (plan), and tactics (actions) and your actions are critical in your case. I've mentioned several tactics previously (Tips are tactics), but they bear mentioning again.

Always have someone with you in the room and recording the meetings. CPS HATES THIS. By recording the conversation, including phone conversations CPS can not threaten directly to "Take the kids" or "We will force you to…" because it comes across as strong-arm tactics and that never looks good in court. This also prevents lying or "misunderstandings." The camera will show what the CPS agent said and will repeat it back precisely; this in court can show the abusive nature of the CPS agent.

Start recording as the CPS worker gets to the house. They will say, "I am not comfortable with being recorded." and will work hard to prevent being recorded. Remember, it is your house, your case and you can record all you like. To the best of my understanding, public officials in the course of executing their positions, do not have a reasonable expectation of privacy, regardless of what they tell you. Child Protective Services may threaten to "terminate the meeting if videoing continues" this is usually an empty threat. CPS wants to get paid and canceling the meeting cuts back on client hours. Also, it can be shown in court that you were willing to meet with CPS to work on issues, but CPS wouldn't work with you. Explaining that to a judge helps to sway them to your side.

I always recommend telling the CPS agent or any public official if and when they are being recorded. It changes the dynamic of the conversation from them having the power to you having the power. If you go online and view videos of CPS interactions, you will see a dramatic shift in personality when the CPS agent knows they are being recorded from when they don't. In Terry's case, just having a third party present prevented any threats or accusations against her, but a video is always better because it never lies or become confused in court.

I also don't recommend going online to find videos similar to your case. Online videos are a tricky situation. Many can show a similar situation as yours but do not reveal the details of the case. Each case is different in its presentation and evidence. It can be a detriment if you use an online video as a guide to your situation. Even if it appears the same, online videos never show the repercussions of the decisions made by parents or CPS agents regarding the abuse they received in the video.

Numerous online videos show people using their 4th amendment rights to keep CPS out of the house or to prevent an investigation.

These are your rights, but as I mentioned earlier, the response is most likely going to be a court order, then they return and force compliance. Refusal to discuss the charges will get you into court, and maybe an emergency removal of children. Removal is entirely legal and should be expected. If they have a suspicion of abuse, they are not going to stop until they thoroughly investigate the situation or take you to court. You'll never see that part of it on YouTube.

Say as little as possible. This tactic includes saying, I don't know, and I prefer not to discuss it. One of tactics CPS use is to get you to relax. Talking about weather, school, work, the lawn and other innocent things will lead to a conversation about the kids and the charges. This technique is useful because once a discussion is started, and rapport is established; it becomes challenging to stop. People will say, "I never meant to talk to her, and I don't know why I did." It is because once you're talking it is difficult to be impolite and say, "I don't want to talk anymore." Sometimes we are talking and don't realize we are talking about it until it is too late.

Threats are a common tactic of Child Protective Services. Calm is called for in these situations. If you were not recording and a CPS worker threatens you, YOU MUST NOT RESPOND EMOTIONALLY. Pretend you didn't hear it or that you do not understand, ask questions like, "what do you mean" and "can you explain why you would do that?" Get them to expand on the threat and maintain being calm. A threat by CPS is a way to test, manipulate and scare. CPS can determine how easily it will be to get you to do what they want by how you react to their threat. Getting them to expand on it can give you several options to get out of the threat as reacting to the threat escalates the issue and forces the threat to become a reality. By saying, "you're threatening to take my kids...why, what have I done to you?" makes the CPS agent have to explain their actions, "You have no evidence for these accusations." calls their bluff, and even when they are bluffing they can often get the court order based on that a statement shows "hostility towards others".

Anger is used as bait for CPS. If they can anger you, they can control you and your actions, to prove you are unfit to have your children. It happened to Dave and Sonya in their situation. Dave lost control based on his illness, and his temper and CPS used it to beat him in court over and over until he was unable to see his daughter anymore. Frank's case would have been much more involved if he became angry with the CPS agent, they would have continued investigating until they went to court and became a permanent fixture in his life. In Terry's case, they would have removed Jordan without just cause or fear of reprisal, and it would have been impossible to get him returned.

Know what you are responsible for and what CPS is accountable. You will be required to sign "Releases of Information" for people to send records to CPS. It is a technical violation of non-self incrimination of the 5th Amendment, but you will have to do it, or they will push the issue in court. However, you do not have to go to the doctor's office, or to the capitol building to get the documents for them. It is still up to them to get the documentation to prove some guilt on their side, not yours. By forcing them to do this, they lose productivity hours and sometimes lose track of what they need for court. By knowing they don't have the documents and asking them to provide them is helpful in court as to disproving their assessment. Don't make it easy for them. They are not there to do you any favors, don't do any for them. If you want to obtain the documents for your case, by all means, but do not do paperwork for CPS, that is their job.

8. CPS Business

Child Protective Services is also a business, just like any other business. Child Protective Services receives a part of its funding from state taxes. However, it has to prove to the state that what it is doing equals or exceeds the budget it was provided in the past few years. This is an important distinction to make. People generally believe CPS have unlimited resources and money for research, evaluation, prosecution, and personnel. This is not the case. Child Protective Services receives some payment based on initial interviews, but mostly their funding is based on open cases and adoptions. Child Protective Services have monetary gains to receive by opening a case on you. By opening the case, and you signing the CPS service plan, they show the state billable hours which transform into funding. From this perspective, CPS has very little to lose and much to gain by providing services to you and your family...and the more services they recommend, the more money CPS can make. Consider Terry and Mark, the main question asked of her thought her nine-month ordeal was, "Please sign the progress plan." At no time did CPS ask to see Jordan or any discernable information regarding him. Child Protective Services didn't care about the welfare of the child, and the CPS agent knew it, so she focused on what her supervisor needed which was to sign the CPS service plan.

Signing the progress plan isn't just a full admission of guilt, it is the way CPS gets paid. Almost all state employees have something similar; police have activity reports to prove they are actively patrolling and how many calls they answer, mental health workers have treatment plans and activity logs of how much client contact was made. Child Protective Services are no different, and they get paid when your case is open and active. It is a systemic problem because if the numbers show a decrease in CPS activity or contact with the public, they are in jeopardy of having their budget reduced. No one in government wants to have their budget cut because it could mean reduction of staff, and no one wants to lose their job. Many CPS agents don't think of it that way; that each person they contact is money. The management, all the way from line supervisor up to the Director of Health and Human Services, does think of it that in that way, and can put undue pressure on the CPS agent to open cases when there isn't a need. I saw it happen in mental health, and it happens in every state-supported field.

Tip #7 Make CPS pay.

CPS is a government agency, but like all government agencies it has a budget to maintain, and not every case is cost effective. As mentioned, CPS receives payment from the state budget plus allocation from the federal budget per child adopted out. Depending on which state you reside, each state allocates different amounts of money to Child Protective Services.

CPS is more likely to fight with low income and low educated people. By focusing on lower-income people, CPS can get more (bang for their buck) so to speak. People who can not afford to fight, or know how to fight, generally cost less to fight because they won't have to deal with motions, injunctions and all the legal maneuverings of an effective attorney. Cost is a factor in which cases CPS becomes involved. It is not the sole factor but a major one. Knowing this, the cost of each case is weighted against its benefit. This means CPS will lose money on a case when it is necessary but will weigh it out case per case. Driving up the cost of the case helps to discourage CPS from continuing the fight, just like it would deter anyone else. Because of this, it is beneficial to file as many motions, injunctions, information requests and subpoenas as possible to CPS. Of course, this will increase your bill with your attorney, and you need to keep your costs in line with your resources, but by doing this, you not only drive up CPS bills but also show you are not an easy target...predators love easy targets. Even if you do not have money to use in court filings, there are smaller things you can use to show you are not going down without a fight. Documents like medical records, SNAP records, financial records etc. are items which CPS will ask you to produce (depending on your case). However, you are not required to provide them. You are only required to sign the release of information for CPS to have access to them. CPS will threaten, "if we don't get these records we will take you to court." But what they want is for you to do the legwork and get the paperwork for them, so they don't have to do "non-billable" paperwork. Billable work is face-to-face contact with the family, while non-billable work includes reports, accessing documents and the like. The State government does this to prevent billing from agents sitting at a desk filling out paperwork and forces the agent into the field to meet with families. By forcing CPS to go to the statehouse to get your IRS Federal tax form, or to the hospital for the medical records, you intrude on their "billable time." It causes the CPS agent to appear less productive, and CPS receives less money as a whole, and the management looks poorly as their overall productivity goes declines. Remember, you must sign the release of information, but when they ask you to go obtain it reply to the CPS agent, "that's your job, not mine." It sounds petty and passive-aggressive, and it is, but it's a way to maintain control over what they access and what they don't.

Do not use rescheduling as a way to avoid or attack CPS. Avoidance can be used against you in court. Child Protective Services will bring up in court the numerous appointments were missed with them, showing a lack of responsibility, and some hostility towards CPS. The court dislikes missed appointments and views this very negatively. Of course, if something authentic comes up, call and reschedule as soon as possible. Make sure you document each rescheduled appointment as to when, where, and why, because your lawyer can refute them. It would not be beneficial for CPS to be arguing medical neglect, then bring up you missing an appointment with them because you took your child to the doctor for a check-up. However, missing a meeting with them without adequate reason looks terrible in court.

First and foremost, always be nice, but always be firm. I mentioned earlier anger, and hostility gets you nowhere with CPS and will be used against you later; a big part of your strategy is to be polite to the CPS agent. Do not mistake it for being weak, or allowing them to do what they want, it means calm and pleasant conversation while being able to say, "no thanks" or "I disagree." When Terry refused to sign the CPS service plan, she said, "no thanks, I don't agree with what's written." Using that in court is difficult. If Terry had said, "Leave!!! I'm not signing that shit!" it would be used to prove her state of mind, and would likely have caused Jordan to be removed from the home before the court hearing. It is always easier to keep the child than to get them back after they've been removed.

Expect at the onset that you are going to court. If you expect you are going to court, it takes the power away from their threat. By assuming the case to go to court, you aren't as easily manipulated by CPS. Going to court is almost a given unless you surrender, so plan accordingly. Plan what you are going to say, prepare your defense, expect to disprove everything they say. Child Protective Services use the threat of court like a mother threatens, "wait until your father gets home." CPS expects you to behave like the judge is going to side with them automatically. Child Protective Services knows the odds are in their favor. CPS understands the pressures they can apply to a family in distress, with extra costs and fear of child removal. Child Protective Services agents do not lose wages, pay for lawyers or gas to and they have nothing personal to lose by taking you to court. Child Protective Services would rather have a court document forcing you than have you comply because you can always change your mind. With a court order, they can walk right past you to do what they want. Which is precisely what you don't want and why you must have a good defense in court.

Identification of the charges is vital to your case. When defending yourself whether in or outside of court, you need to know what the charges are and what CPS wants to accomplish. The charges are on the CPS service plan they will demand you to sign. Charges will usually be on the first or second page, often followed by diagnostic numbers. Once you know the charges, you can determine what evidence you will need to proceed with the case. It is vital to provide third party evidence to CPS and court of the alternate possibility or impossibility of every action they are accusing. Evidence such as scheduled physicians' appointments if they're citing medical neglect, psychological assessment if they are citing mental illness, Women Infant, and Children (WIC) appointments if they are accusing malnutrition. Each case is different, but there is usually a way to disprove the accusations of CPS. This does not mean they won't take it to court, but it does mean you have a better chance to come away with your children and get CPS out of your life. Proving your innocence isn't something people consider when entering a courtroom, but as stated earlier the burden of proof in CPS/Family court "guilty until proven innocent."

Without knowing the charges, you go into court blind, as I did in Dave's case. I knew he was not violent, but I didn't know the exact charges. Without that, I couldn't disprove anything CPS was accusing. I presented my best psychiatric case, but I was using a scatter presentation when a CPS defense needs to be precise. If I could have redirected back to how his behavior was due to bipolar disorder versus his personality, I believe he would have had a better chance of reconnecting with his family. By presenting his behavior as a controlled medical condition, and can be stated the likelihood of it reoccurring is slim.

I believe the saddest mistake people make in family court is believe in is the judge will see them, talk to them, know how much they love their children, and understand they are doing the best they can for the children and dismiss the charges....and that never happens. Hypothetically, let's say they accuse medical neglect like in Frank's case. You can come into court and show how much you love your children, how much you work for their benefit, but if you don't address the charges you are going to have CPS in your life for years, and lose your child.

Plan exactly how you are going to address each of the charges, and find evidence discrediting each charge. Do not leave any charges on the table as it will come back to haunt you. Child Protective Services may push for multiple charges, two big ones, and a small one. This is done to overwhelm you with the more significant charges so they can sneak in with the smaller one. Remember, the business side of CPS, open cases make money. Regardless of what charges are presented, whether severe or minuscule, open cases is their goal.

Most cases by CPS are "he said, she said" without any true evidence to back up either side. When this happens, CPS always wins. I've witnessed this first hand in Dave's case and viewed cases similar online. Child Protective Services uses language like, "it is our opinion" and "our doctor recommends." These are statements used to persuade the judge that it is a group effort. Questioning of these statements is critical in a case, such as "Did the doctor meet with the defendant?. How many people met with the defendant to make this determination or diagnosis?"

The CPS agent is not a lawyer and usually is not a proficient witness. I was easily tripped up on the stand, by simple language. The CPS agent typically has a Bachelor's degree in mental health, social work or similar background. Question them in court about how they came to this determination for diagnosis, testing, and methodologies used to validate their opinion. Most CPS agents are not the person who decides to move forward, and it catches them off guard to ask them questions they can not answer. Saying, "Because my supervisor told me to" isn't acceptable in court. The CPS agent is supposed to be the expert in your case and by showing they don't know the reasoning behind the diagnosis or claim will go a long way to leveling the playing field. Don't rely on only this, even if you ultimately discredit the CPS agent, the weight of evidence is still 51/49 in their favor, due to expert bias.

Surrender is never an option. By surrendering to CPS, the agent will eventually set you up for failure and the loss of your children. Child Protective Services is a very patient organization. The agents know that in the long term they can set up stumbling blocks leading to taking children away. It can give directives to go to counseling or AA/NA and then decide the interventions are not sufficient and remove the children from their parents. I have researched numerous cases of children being removed from their homes for one reason or another, and it is near impossible to regain custody of your children once they are removed from the home. It is possible to get them back, but once they are removed, it is extremely difficult to get them back. CPS does not want to return them because they will lose money in the case. They will use, "child has acclimated at the new residence, it would be traumatic to uproot and return to parents." CPS will file motion after motion for any reason and will string along the parent until the situation becomes hopeless, and the parents have no choice but to surrender.

Working with CPS doesn't need to be considered a failure, but an alternative solution. If CPS provides a simple, direct way to have CPS out of your life, take it. If the intervention is minimal and not invasive to your life like, "see a nutritionist once a month," and they agree they will discontinue service after straightforward and clear goals are met, then that should be your focus. The easier and cheaper way to get them out of your life should be the goal. Always receive the agreement in writing. Record or video everything. This is because CPS can rescind or change their minds regarding your case (which they do to collect more money from the state). You then can bring the evidence to the court and convince the judge of their dishonesty. Every agreement should be in writing and video.

9. Online evidence.

If I were a superstitious person, I could rationalize these issues as bad luck, that for some reason I always come across a problem CPS agent. However, after researching online, I've found numerous other problems regarding CPS, including abuse, neglect, and sex trafficking. I found data which suggests the removal of a child by CPS is in some cases more traumatic than the abuse they receive at home. According to the Providence Journal:

[In one Pawtucket home, an employee used the agency van to help run a teenage sex-trafficking operation, prosecutors allege.

* At a Providence home, a worker drove the company van to North Providence to taxi a 16-year-old girl with autism — who had been reported missing to police — back to the all-male group home. When child-welfare investigators visited the home where the girl stayed the night, they found the building reeking of marijuana, a bedroom littered with garbage and condoms, little food, and a maintenance man left in charge.]

[A redacted report by the state Office of the Child Advocate to the Department of Children, Youth & Families on an incident July 28, when a resident of a Providence group home suffered paralysis and required emergency spine surgery after taking a fall during a reportedly unauthorized outing to a trampoline park. Child welfare officials have questioned why the 17-year-old boy was at the children's park, where he reportedly had been injured once before; the home lacked permission from his mother or a state supervisor.} [The Providence Journal / Sandor Bodo]

[Last March a woman told police her 16-year-old foster daughter was missing. A worker from this Whitmarsh Corp. group home had picked her up in North Providence and brought her back to the home, where she spent the night with her 20-year-old boyfriend.] [The Providence Journal / Kris Craig]

[During a late-night argument, a former worker in this Child and Family Services group home allegedly ordered two teenage female residents outside, where they were assaulted by his girlfriend.} [The Providence Journal / Kris Craig]

[The recommendations by the state Office of the Child Advocate to the Department of Children, Youth & Families about one of the state's group-home operators note that "[Whitmarsh] staff admittedly falsified documentation and left youth alone and unattended for *extended periods of time and relied on a maintenance worker to provide staff coverage." As a response in cases of staff members assaulting residents, the report says, "the Whitmarsh administration simply moves the perpetrator to a different location." [The Providence Journal / Sandor Bodo]*

At least four times in the last five months (in 2017), *workers at state-regulated group homes took actions that left young people in their care hospitalized, endangered or exploited, a Providence Journal investigation has found.*

In two cases, group-home employees attempted to cover up slack supervision and management with forged log books or falsified statements, investigators reported. Meanwhile, all four homes remain open under the auspices of the Department of Children, Youth & Families.]

It is possible to conceive the removal of a child from a household as a form of trauma. Considering when a child is abused, there is a crime being committed. When abuse occurs, it would be more beneficial to arrest the abuser rather than the abused. Removing the child punishes the child for being abused and traumatizes the child even more significant than the original abuse. If a burglar is in a store, you don't remove the store clerk for his safety. You remove the burglar because he committed the crime. However, in the CPS system, removal of the child is the standard action to a threat, not the removal of the parent. By removing the child, the child perceives himself/herself as the guilty party which can traumatize them even more than the abuse itself. Removing a child from the home causes anxiety, depression, separation and attachment issues which cause an increase in psychiatric services and the likelihood of legal problems including incarceration as an adult. According to the Juvenile Law Resource Center (www.youthrightsjustice.org), :

[Theoretical research and expert opinion indicate that removing a child from the home causes serious trauma. Though informative, these findings are categorically different from the empirical studies discussed later in this article which actually examine outcomes for large groups of children placed in foster care. Many sources

acknowledge that separating a child from a parent for even a relatively short time can have a devastating emotional and physical impact on the child.

For some children, separations may be experienced as a significant rejection or loss that affects the formation of attachments. Children who are removed from parents often come to expect parental unavailability, which distorts adjustment to surrogate caregivers and the foster home environment.

Experts also note that disruptions in the parent-child relationship may "provoke fear and anxiety in a child and diminish his or her sense of stability and self." Using the Harm of Removal and Placement to Advocate for Parent Clients (rev. 1/7/10) Thus by removing children from parents, removal undermines children's attachments, identity, and subsequent caregiving relationships. For children in homes where there is domestic violence, the consequences of removal to foster care can be more severe. One court noted expert testimony that "if a child is placed in foster care as a result of domestic violence in the home, he or she may view such removal as a traumatic act of punishment… and [think] that something [the mother] has done or failed to do has caused this separation."

Additionally, for children already experiencing separation anxiety, removal from a battered parent's custody will serve to further intensify those feelings by interrupting a positive attachment to the non-abusing parent. Another expert concluded the removal heightens the child's sense of self-blame, and that children exposed to domestic violence are at a significantly above normal risk of suffering separation anxiety disorder if separated from their mother.]

Child Protective Services has a specific job to do, "protect the welfare and safety of children." It is a noble and challenging job as no one knows what the future holds or how someone is going to behave in every situation. Child Protective Services is supposed to take each case, person by person, step by step, to minimize damage to children while providing support of families. However as we have seen, in some cases, they have become more law enforcement than social work, when they remove a child for safety the placement may be worse than the home, and they allow their emotional opinions or personal agendas drive the outcome.

10. Adoption and Child Safety Act 1997

I wanted to detail some of the ideas in the Adoptions and Child Safety Act of 1997 (H.R.867) Public Law 105-89, which I believe to be a direct cause of the current destruction of families and overreach of CPS. I used some information from www.naswdc.org or the National Association of Social Workers in Washington DC. The four main provisions mentioned are: Shorten the time frame for the child's first permanency hearing, offers financial incentives for increasing the number of adoptions, sets new requirements for termination of parental rights and reauthorizes the Family Preservation and Support act.

The parts of this Law which need addressing are the financial incentives to remove children from their homes and the requirements to terminate parental rights. Under this law, there is an "adoption incentive payment of $4000 for each adoption of a foster child above the base number (unknown), plus another $2000 for children with special needs. Special needs can be anything from a dietary restriction to traumatic brain injury. Imagine any other public service receiving special funding for each action they perform. Those specific actions would dramatically increase. It is basic psychology; any reward strengthens the behavior targeted. If police agencies were given $1000 for every federal charge brought, eventually every crime would be a federal crime. Likewise, if the fire department were offered $1000 for every arson detected, every fire would be arson until proved otherwise.

The point I'm making is that, when you give incentives for certain actions to occur, they will increase in frequency, and when it comes to removing children from their families and adopting them out, it becomes something very vicious and cruel. It becomes a pay for children system where the more children you move from one family to another the more money is made. Almost sounds like slavery in the 1700's, where the more people placed on a boat heading to the new world, the more people they could sell at auction. It is not far from that concept.

This type of incentive system should never be used in public service, not just for the abuse it creates to obtain funding from the federal government, but also the violations it causes with human rights and civil liberties. The children adopted out are not from middle to upper-income families with money to use on defense and lawyers. Most are from lower-income households who can not afford to defend themselves without sacrificing the basics like food. Unlike criminal court, you generally do not get a state-appointed lawyer to help defend you, and CPS relies on this.

The National Association of Social Workers in District of Columbia website (NASWDC.org) directly states the federal government provides technical assistance for "encouraged use of fast-tracking for children under age one into pre-adoptive placements; and programs to place children into pre-adoptive placements before termination of parental rights.". Meaning, Child Protective Services is to start placing a child into adoptive care while the parent still has rights to the child.

Under the Adoptions and Child Safety Act, "States must continue to make reasonable effort to preserve and reunify families. However, the reasonable effort requirement does not apply in all cases". In short, if the child is suffering from abuse, parent assaulted another child, or if other siblings have been permanently removed, CPS no longer has to make "reasonable efforts" to reunify the family. "Reasonable efforts" is a difficult term to define. "Reasonable" in legal language means, "what the general public would consider as prudent." However, "reasonable" in all CPS cases are determined by CPS, with no oversight from another department, court, or facility.

The CPS system is designed to set people up to have their children removed based on little more than a phone call, pays CPS $4000 per child to adopt out, gives little to no defense to the parent, zero oversight, and no penalty for mistakes or errors. This provides every reason to remove children and no reason to keep the family intact.

While researching, I had contact with a lady whose grandchildren were adopted out by CPS. Her story shows how little regard CPS has for maintaining family continuity. Sara is a +55-year-old woman who lost her grandchild. Sara's daughter wasn't feeding the child enough through breastfeeding (a common occurrence) and the child was wasting away. By the time Sara got her granddaughter to the hospital the child had passed away. A devastating story in itself, but then CPS became involved.

Once they began investigating the death of the child, CPS decided to remove both of Sara's other grandchildren from their mother for their safety, even though there was nothing physically or emotionally wrong with the children, and they were eating solid foods. Child Protective Service, instead of finding a family member (like Sara) who the children could stay with while the investigation continued, placed the children into foster care. By placing them in foster care instead of an alternate family member's care, they started the clock on when they could adopt the children out. This falls under the reasonable efforts exemption clause of the Adoption and Child Safety Act. Then before Sara could do anything about it, the kids were away in foster care regardless of Sara's assurances, or her ability to prove she maintained a safe household. Child Protective

Services denied Sara because she had asked CPS for help in the past. Fifteen years prior, Sara requested assistance from CPS regarding guidance of her child. Child Protective Services used this single contact to deem Sara an unfit placement for the children, for nothing more than a fifteen-year-old phone call.

Sara's daughter did obtain a pro bono attorney. However, the attorney wasn't much help to either Sara's daughter or Sara as he was simultaneously working on both Sara's daughter's legal case from the death of her daughter and the family court case. Even in accidental death cases, the courts press charges to determine negligence. It took all of twenty minutes in family court to dissolve all parental rights of Sara's daughter. Despite the mandate of maintaining the family, and not having been convicted of a crime, CPS adopted the children out to the foster family they were using, even after official requests were made to the court for Sara to have custody. No consideration was given by CPS to give custody to Sara, no consideration to the rest of the family, just the payment of two $4000 stipends from the federal government to enhance their budget.

The law initially designed to assist children in need is being abused by state governments to increase their allotment of the 325 million dollars (FY2001) allocated to the Adoption and Child Safety Act. They are tearing families apart to adopt children out using the vague and manipulability terms "Reasonable efforts" and no oversight into the decisions of CPS.

The point with this is twofold. Understand what you are fighting against; how much CPS stand to gain from the fight and how the current law is set up against the common good of the people. Does it benefit the sibling children to be taken away from their parents because of an accidental death? It depends on the situation. However, I am sure removing the children and not placing them in a safe family member home is not in the best interest of the family, only the best interest of CPS and its budget.

11. Court Abuses

Removing a child from his/her parent with nothing more than an opinion from a social worker and an informal hearing from a family court judge is unconscionable. It is a direct violation of human rights. Destroying the family for money, power or politics should never be allowed or condoned in a free society. To do so with such little oversight and legal effort on the grounds of the state is overreach at a minimum and oppressive.

The most egregious violation of CPS and the family court system is the nullification of rights, whether parental, civil or natural rights without due process of law. Child Protective Services and the family court attempt to present as a fair and balanced system. This system, which primarily focuses on the poor and undereducated, then removes children without benefit of a trial or even a court-appointed attorney, is nothing short of a kangaroo court. Any court where the government brings charges, the accused is required to spend money they don't have, on an accusation made from an anonymous source, where the accused must provide information to the government, and prove innocence over the presumption of guilt is more relatable to North Korea than the United States of America.

But this is the standard in the Family Court in America.

In no other American court is the violation and removal of rights allowed without a lawyer being present to defend the accused. In no other court is the Constitution as blatantly ignored. In no other court is the process of law so easily forgotten. Under the guise of "child welfare" or " best interest of the child" even the child's rights and needs are denied because of nothing more than CPS opinion.

My recommendation to repair family court is to treat the defendant similar as to a criminal court proceeding, including court attorneys for each side, and full protection under the 4th, 5th, 6th and 8th amendments.

Having these rights reinstated and enforced will help the court process through what are real cases for having rights nullified versus a money play by CPS. The court system would then be able to process evidence without the bias displayed currently.

This seems like a small item, but reform of the family court system is monumental. Most judges in family court are oblivious to their own bias, and worse are the arbiters of their prejudices. Few judges recuse themselves in the face of conflicts of interest, fewer acknowledge having any biases in their judgment. Family court is the worst for bias, as mentioned earlier the judge considers CPS' opinion over all else in the court. By disposing of that bias, the system would begin to protect the family versus safeguarding CPS budget.

The bias in family court has become so problematic that providing false evidence has become commonplace. In December 2016, the 9th district court of Appeals heard an argument by CPS stating that CPS should be allowed to falsify evidence to the court in order to present a better case and accelerate family child removal. In the case, Hardwick v. Marcia Vreeken, case #15-55563, revolved around whether or not CPS should be allowed to lie in court for their means. Not an argument about whether or not CPS had provided false evidence, they fully admitted to falsifying evidence in the case, the argument is about whether or not they are allowed to do so in a court of law. The part which amazed me was, the three judges went on recess to consider the argument. The 9th district court of appeals was considering whether or not an agency of the state is allowed to falsify evidence to a court of law, to promote the violation of the right of parenthood. The ramification of this is painfully apparent. Once CPS has been contacted, they would be able to present any information to the court, whether real or false, to substantiate their claims. The case is located online, Hardwick v Marcia Vreeken case number 15-55563. This is a direct connection to how biased the Child Protective Service system has become regarding the family. CPS considers itself above the constitution. These are severe charges, and I suggest watching the video rather than taking my word for it.

The implications of Hardwick v Vreeken are astounding. Child Protective Services would be able to come to your house, based on a call from an anonymous source. Then lie to the judge to remove the child by force (with police assistance). When in court the mother, who may not be able to afford legal counsel, has to defend herself not just from fact but false evidence presented to the court. In this system, how does one receive justice? How is it possible to protect yourself from an anonymous phone call, which could be a mistake or the names were confused? It is impossible to give any clear or rational defense in these situations. But these are everyday situations across America.

Luckily, the Ninth Circuit Court of Appeals came back with a ruling on January 3, 2017. The court ruled that CPS could not use its immunity to commit perjury and manufacture evidence to remove children from home. Legal violations are so commonplace, the Ninth District Circuit Court of Appeals (same court as in Hardwick v. Vreeken) has stated from a separate case, Camerta v. Greene, where CPS entered a school, interviewed a child regarding sexual abuse without any parent, and removed the child from the family without a court order. The details of the court hearing are of sexual misconduct with a boy not related to him. Later it was suggested he molested his daughter. After a mistrial, the man pleaded "no contest" to the charges and sentenced accordingly. However, even in such a horrendous case, numerous violations of law plagued the case including violations of the 4th amendment, no judicial oversight, and questionable evidence. The appellate court stated in their findings:

[*the court held the seizure under these circumstances violated the fourth Amendment", "Several Circuit courts have found Child Protective Services Agents are the functional equivalent of police officers conducting such investigations and should, therefore, be governed by the same Fourth Amendment standards", "The juvenile dependency system in this country is dysfunctional", "Justice Carlos Moreno of the California Supreme Court has noted the system is in need of a major overhaul"," The problem stems in part from CPS agents lack proper education, training, accountability, and oversight. An unwarranted intrusion upon a family may be as devastating to a child as any failure to act in a case of severe abuse." "Through misuse of this power- whether intentional or negligent, social services agencies have become feared institutions in the minds of many Americans. This compels adoption of constitutional standards adequate to ensure CPS agents and police officers carry out their mandate to protect children and preserve families where possible- without denigrating the rights they are charged to protect". "Judicial review is essential in the* absence of an emergency or parental consent." "Experience demonstrates that when CPS agents and the police or sheriffs investigating alleged child abuse bypass judicial review, violations of constitutional rights of children and parents often occur." "Allowing CPS agents and policemen to interview children at school in the absence of exigency, parental consent or a warrant as Petitioners urge, will undoubtedly lead to many more abuses of families." "The Joining of forces by CAPTA, between CPS agents and police creates doctrinal confusion under the Fourth Amendment because of the mixed motives of government officials." "One could surmise the only reason these agents went to the school to interrogate this little girl was they were trying to skirt the constitutional warrant." "This has become a widespread practice among police and CPS agents." "No remedy exists in the juvenile courts for abuse of Constitutional rights." "The vast majority of CPS agents lack the education and training to qualify as a "professional." "Other systemic issues illustrate the need for a check on the power of CPS agents." "The government's vital interest in preventing child abuse does not require sacrifice of Fourth Amendment protections." "Money creates a perverse incentive in the juvenile system" "Since the funding is tied to the removal and adoption of children, little *effort is made to keep children at home with services to the parents. The longer the child remains out of the home, the more money CPS agencies receive." "This funding under Title IV-E of the Social Security Act has spawned a huge child abuse industry." "It is the function of a neutral magistrate, not CPS agent, to determine what constitutes probable cause as required by the Fourth Amendment."]* (from Change.org)

11. Improvement Possibilities

Condemnations from the Ninth Circuit Court of Appeals regarding Child Protective Services suggest there is the opportunity for improvement, Justice Carlos Moreno does bring up some fascinating points. There are ways to fix the system to decrease the need for removing the children from their homes, more repairs to reduce false positives and having children removed and adopted without need. These changes would need to be broad measures among all states and court systems. The best solution to the issue would be to remove the payment for adopting out and change CPS to focus on providing social services to the families instead of punishments, threats, court, and civil rights violations by abducting children.

Taking the reward out of the adoption factor will change the focus directly from revenue gains to family assistance, where it should have been all along. Removal or restructuring of the 1997 Adoption and Child Safety Act would be a great place to start.

The system would benefit from independent legal oversight from an outside agency. Hospitals, healthcare organizations, doctors offices and the like have accreditation standards to do the work regarding healthcare. The Joint Commission on Accreditation of Healthcare Organizations, (JCAHO) oversees healthcare organizations to lessen the number of errors in healthcare. Hospitals which use this system routinely review for errors, mistakes, and problems with the system and systematically reform any system which becomes problematic. Having worked in the psychiatric realm, I've seen patient care not just improve from this kind of system, but the overall organization improves. Having an outside organization review cases and discuss problems within the system limits the amount of corruption that can be developed by poor performance practices, personality judgments, and incompetence. An outside agency as a review system can point out ineffective operations, legal issues, policies, and in my opinion should be conducted every time a child is removed from the home as a part of the safety protocols.

Currently, Child Protective Services is relying on the judgment of one to two poorly trained social workers and an overworked area manager to decide the fate of a child. The evidence should be reported to a neutral third party outside of the court system for approval before removing any child, except in emergency situations of imminent threat. One possibility would be to have an outside party such as an ombudsman or arbitrator review the facts before court. Judges tend to side with CPS when contacted, receive only partial information, and do not have time to review all necessary information required to make such a drastic and ultimately destructive decision. They become biased by making these decisions without all the relevant information for the task, nor should they be required to perform this action.

Second, once a judge makes a decision, that's the decision, and each side is required to abide by that decision. Once they remove the child from the household, the judge is automatically biased to stay with his or her decision instead of admitting their decision was incorrect or misguided by erroneous information. This hubris is observable in numerous courtrooms across the nation. The judge should not be swayed by any prior knowledge during a family court hearing, and a preview of a written emergency removal warrant certainly conflicts with the court's neutrality. Even if the presiding judge isn't the person who signed the Temporary Removal Order, it is unlikely one judge will go against another judge's decision due to professional courtesy and legal conflict.

Child Protective Services has quasi-police powers. This has to be reformed. Police spend nearly a year in classes to learn about proper arrest procedure, rights, police powers, and limitations. They usually spend 1-2 years under the guidance of a veteran of the police department before being able to work independently, (different agencies have different guidelines, but in general this is standard). Child Protective Services has no such training when it comes to policy, procedures, rights, powers or limitations. Child Protective Services uses on the job training, usually lasting two weeks to 30 days (again, different agencies have different practices), and may or may not require a college degree in social work, mental health or related field to practice in the field. There is no licensing requirement to be a CPS agent, no revoking of license for malpractice, ethics violations or illegal behavior. Most illegal practice is managed by the manager of the department and in more extreme cases human resources.

To remedy this Child Protective Services must be either held to the same standards of full police powers under the law, with the same judicial limitations and training requirements as the police, or they should be given no prosecutorial powers. By having no prosecutorial powers CPS would have to use the criminal court system with the same requirements for guilt and sentencing as a victim of a crime, the difference being that CPS would be an advocate for the child instead of the agency bringing charges and providing lawyers prosecution.

If given no prosecution powers, Child Protective Services' role should be changed from family overseer to family assistance. The difference would be quite striking. CPS culture would change from a punishment view of "do this or I will take your child" to "let us work on this to better your life and your child." By acting as a family advocate, CPS could use its network to assist parents into substance abuse classes, parenting classes, connect with food and housing placement, review parental progress and the overall health and well-being of the child. Social work would be a better use of the CPS agents' time than waiting in the halls of a courthouse waiting to testify as to why a child should be adopted out.

It is unfair and to remove rights without a trial. Court hearings are insufficient to manage such issues. Hearings are beneficial if parents are reluctant to treatment or there is a conflict between the parent and Child Protective Services. However, during a trial where the rights are in jeopardy, an attorney should be provided by the state, at a minimum. Private attorneys are always a possibility. However, when a private attorney is unattainable by the parent, a public defender should be in place. As in the case of Dave and

Sonya, without an attorney, it was impossible to get a fair hearing. Dave had no idea what, when or how to ask questions, how to present a defense and even with evidence presented of his acknowledgment of a problem and participation in treatment, he remained separate from his wife and child due to legal maneuvering. It would take one public defender, and one public prosecutor to be assigned to the family court to alleviate this gross misalignment of due process. By having attorneys on both sides, this would provide a proper balance of evidence to the presiding judge.

Even if the person is recorded on camera, was caught with direct evidence and admitted to performing the crime, in America, the accused must stand trial before being sentenced to incarceration, removal of property or nullification of rights. This is constitutional law, and the judicial system balances this daily. Included in the trial is a review of the evidence, safeguards against tainted evidence, alternative possibilities of the crime and a lawyer provided if one can not afford one. None of these are provided in the family court system, and the most direct way to positively change this system would be to offer the similar protections in family court as in criminal court. Children are our most valuable possession. When a child is removed with only as much as an informal hearing, with no attorney, and no evidence, it damages the legal system as much as the child. Parental rights are rights. They should be as protected as your choice of religion, your freedom to speak, your vote, travel, etc.

An overall CPS/Social Services system change is required to revise the social service system. Some states are making minimal changes. These are mostly cosmetic. The system in every state should be transformed from a police agency to a social service system. This would entail Child Protective Services having direct and immediate access to mental health services, anger management classes, substance abuse treatment (inpatient and outpatient), food banks, and housing services. By making CPS a direct conduit into receiving services, we can decrease the child removal system we have currently and replace it with support and care.

Currently, the methodology for treatment and care in CPS are threats and coercion. Parents who are in need of services are required to find their way through the social service system. Having worked in the system for over almost two decades, I can say with all certainty that no one can possibly manage the system without assistance. When you add mental illness, drugs, CPS pressures, inadequate housing or no food, it is evident that the demands required by Child Protective Services are unreasonable at any level, and usually are set up as roadblocks to retaining or regaining parental rights.

Accessing services requires a high level of bureaucratic skill and salesmanship, of which even many social workers lack, let alone someone who has never been in the system. Coupling this lack of knowledge with the lack of available services dooms the child and parent to separation. Numerous accounts have been relayed to me regarding children being removed from households due to substance abuse issues. In many, the parent was either unable to access the services, unable to pay for services, or was not able to access the proper services in the time required by Child Protective

Services, with disastrous results. By making Child Protective Services a direct conduit to these social services, the parents who are trying to follow CPS recommendations would be able to progress with their treatment rather than be set on a hopeless task which is bound to fail.

By requiring state funding to drug rehab and mental health treatment centers be partially based on CPS recommendations, the system refocuses from an affordability system to a needs-based system. The money used for court hearings and other interventions could be directed towards treatment centers. People who require treatment to maintain custody of their children would have some treatment to stabilize their condition, learn about their issues, learn how to manage symptoms and problems, learn how to manage better in society and be able to maintain custody of their children. This will directly lower costs by decreasing the need for foster care, alternative housing, and psychiatric services for the children by being traumatized by removing them from their parents, for years to come. Similar to home psychiatric services for the severely mentally ill, providing home services through Child Protective Services lowers costs significantly, due to decreasing 24-hour care systems, housing and the like. This would also increase direct care and observation of the parent/child relationship and, as providing this type of assistance would demonstrate the sincerity and desire of the parent to either participate in treatment or be used as evidence of an inability to provide care. Removal of at-risk children for safety reasons would be appropriate only if after coordinated care had been attempted and failed. Proof of a parent unwilling or unable to stay in treatment would be direct evidence to the court of the inability of the parent to prioritize the children over themselves. At that point, Child Protective Services could present it to the court as evidence of the failure of the parent versus an inability to access care. This removes much of the opinion issue regarding the court hearing by showing direct evidence of intervention and failure, instead of the opinion of a CPS agent. Judges in the family court system would no longer need to base their findings on the testimony of one CPS agent vs. the testimony of a stressed-out parent with social problems, but a fair attempt to reconcile the social issues with proper care and the ability or inability of the parent to actively participate in services.

I envision a scenario where, when a CPS agent receives notice of possible issues they investigate, the investigation is about connecting people to the services they need rather than threatening changes CPS require and waiting for the parent to cooperate or fail. CPS would render assistance more as a paramedic rather than police, where we try to solve the social problem in the household instead of criminalizing it.

Of course, if there is an imminent issue of safety, the child would need to be removed from the household. However, the goal would be to reunite the parent and child as the parent connects with services in addition to CPS visits, and the connection to treatment be enough to reconnect the parent and child. As noted in the Adoption and Child Safety Act, adoption after 'reasonable attempt of reconciliation' is attempted. It is unreasonable for CPS to consider it a 'reasonable attempt' for any individual who is unable to manage the vast bureaucracy, obtain treatment due to financial constraints or unavailability of said treatment to have 'reasonably attempted' and failed because the requirements of CPS were unavailable or unattainable. If the behaviors continue after being connected to the proper services are being rendered, it shows again the direct lack of ability to place the child's needs ahead of their own and permanent removal is required, but only after all other avenues have been exhausted.

Training, education and licensing should be a prime focus of Child Protective Services. As I mentioned before, navigating the social service bureaucracy is daunting. In the social service system, there are many obstacles where politics get more results than process. The CPS agent would need training regarding what paperwork is required for each agency, how to open cases with other agencies, and what requirements are necessary to connect the parent with service.

Currently, there is little to no training for outside agency documentation. It's a learn as you go process, and with such an enormous task most are unable to manage it. I used a personal system to navigate the bureaucracy, where I would befriend an agent in each agency (social security, Medicaid, food banks, etc.) then when there was a problem I would go to that person to ask for advice or help in the situation. It dramatically decreased the confusion of who to contact, and I was able to get simple, direct answers to very complex problems and expedite the process. One of the most common complaints I received from service agencies is incomplete applications. This wastes the social worker's time by having to decline documents due to errors or incomplete applications, then having to return them hoping the next time they see the application it is complete. By connecting with the agent, the process becomes easier to complete in its entirety and moves on which reduces workloads on already overworked people.

To improve care, Child Protective Services would need a single contact focused on accessing social service care to each outside agency. The agent would be trained to manage all agency paperwork and contacts, but CPS would be sent directly to them to expedite the process and reduce rejection for incomplete applications and services.

Lastly, to improve the Child Protection Service system, legal liability should be a requirement. Currently, 36 states in the U.S. provide immunity for the CPS agent acting under the agency banner. This is an opening for abuse. With immunity in place, violations of the law cannot be prosecuted or managed in civil court. The complaint would be directed to CPS as an organization. It is difficult to receive remedy as the organization would deny responsibility, cannot be criminally charged and can remove the agent from the position which will appear as a remedy but doesn't repair the damages to the parent, child or family, as well as doesn't educate CPS or the agent regarding the infraction. By placing some legal liability on CPS and its agents, we can decrease strong-arm tactics and legal infringements upon families. People behave differently when they have a legal liability, and they become careful about what is communicated, cautious about their techniques and diligent to follow standards of care. This is observable in nursing care where a violation of standards of care can not just end a job, but a career by losing licensure. Having worked with nurses, they taught that the standard of care is ultimately the focus of treatment, and by focusing on the standard of care fewer mistakes are made, and outcomes improve. Legal liability should always be present when decisions are made, and supervision is required when questions arise. Child Protective Services agents should be held to a similar requirement, as the violation of the standard of care for CPS can be just as dire.

In Terry's case, having some liability of the decisions made might have diverted the personal interests of the medical director, having her rethink whether the breach in ethics and the breach of law would be worth risking her career, and provide a path for recourse against such an egregious violation of power.

Child Protective Services has the potential to become a model of efficiency, standards, and treatment for people with social issues and problems. By implementing just a few of the recommendations provided in this book CPS could restructure itself from an agency of force, fear, and intimidation to an agency of treatment and well being. By changing the culture of the agency from policing to social work, the dynamic of the agency and its interactions with 'at risk' parents transforms from coercion to cooperation and threats and obstacles to assistance and guidance. By assisting parents, improved conditions are made for not just the child, but the family unit as a whole, which should be the goal for all social service agencies across America.

www.ingramcontent.com/pod-product-compliance
Lightning Source LLC
Chambersburg PA
CBHW031923240526
45464CB00022B/668